Patterns of Sound SERIES

The Choral Approach t

Sight-Singing

for 3-Part Mixed Voices

VOLUME II

by
Emily Crocker
and
Joyce Eilers

- More complete a cappella and accompanied songs
- More challenging rhythms
- Melodic exercises with bigger skips and more variety
- Songs and exercises using accidentals
- Songs and exercises and chord drills in minor keys
- Introduction to songs with modulations
- And much more!!!

Exclusively Distributed By
HAL•LEONARD® CORPORATION
7777 W. Bluemound Rd. P.O. Box 13819 Milwaukee, WI 53213

THE CHORAL APPROACH TO SIGHT-SINGING, VOLUME II

TABLE OF CONTENTS

* Accompanied Song

TEACHER'S GUIDE

What Is Three-Part Mixed?

One of the interesting developments in middle school and junior high music education programs in the past few years has been the evolution of the three-part mixed choir. In many cases there has been an enrollment drop among boys due to scheduling difficulties and other conflicts. Often, the few boys who do enroll are an interesting combination of totally unchanged voices, totally changed voices, and some voices which are in the process of changing. Yet, these boys, though few in number, have a social need to sit together and sing the same part.

Regular SAB music is often too low for the unchanged and changing voices, and the result is a large gap between the alto and the baritone part. SSA music is totally out of range for the changed voices and often has feminine qualities. Two-part music doesn't make sufficient use of the talent in the upper voices and neither Part I or Part II can accommodate the changing voice.

The answer for many choirs has been Three-Part Mixed music, which uses a **compromise range** for Part III. It is notated in bass clef to stress the masculine aspect of the music, although it is usually within the range of many female altos. The range is very limited:

with an occasionally optional note above or below. Limited as it is, it is not ideal, as it is too high for the totally changed voices, too low for the totally unchanged voices, but it is generally just right for those voices which are enroute. While it is not perfect, it is possible.

Understandably, any choral conductor would prefer to work with an SATB group, but if the group has few boys, or if they don't have the adequate range or experience for SATB music, three-part mixed music can be the answer. Additionally the singers can gain the confidence and experience to eventually move on to more challenging material.

If you have found the need to use this voicing, **THE CHORAL APPROACH TO SIGHT-SINGING** will help you teach your students to sight-read. If your students have used **PATTERNS OF SOUND Sight-Singing Course For Young Singers** by Joyce Eilers and Emily Crocker, **THE CHORAL APPROACH TO SIGHT-SINGING** is a logical extension for the middle school/junior high singer whose voice is beginning to mature. If, however, your students are beginning sight-singers, **THE CHORAL APPROACH TO SIGHT-SINGING** starts from square one, assuming no previous training. It's logical design and easy-to-use format help produce quick results. Three-part harmony is introduced through combinable exercises, which produce rhythmic and melodic independence.

One of the important features of this method is the use of "real songs" which help relate the process of sight-reading to "real music." These songs, both a cappella and accompanied, occur at certain points throughout the book, and serve to reinforce the musical concepts that have been introduced in the exercises. These songs become "intrinsic rewards" and are usually anticipated with great enthusiasm by the students.

Your students' skills will grow by leaps and bounds. Success breeds succeeds - for all students, not just the gifted few. The potential for real musicality in your young singers is tremendous and this method is designed to help them achieve it. We hope you will find the path to musical literacy to be equally satisfying for both you and your students.

Course Overview

Volume I: Rhythmic concepts include quarter, half, dotted half, whole notes and rests; eighth notes and rests; dotted quarter/eighth patterns; 4/4, 3/4, 2/4 meters; ties and slurs. **Melodic concepts** include songs and exercises in the major keys of G, C, F, B flat, D, A, E flat, A flat; how to find "do" in any key. **Harmonic concepts** include introduction to 3-part singing, combinable exercises, 12 songs (a cappella and accompanied) chord progressions (including an optional bass part) and interval practice in the I, IV, and V chords.

Volume II: Rhythmic concepts include syncopation, sixteenth notes, dotted rhythms, 6/8. **Melodic concepts** include more challenging melodic exercises with larger intervals and more variety; accidentals, minor keys, and modulations. **Harmonic concepts** include more a cappella and accompanied songs (many with an optional bass part) and minor key chord progressions.
THE CHORAL APPROACH TO SIGHT-SINGING has been developed using the rhythm syllables popularized by Kodaly and Orff teachers, and the movable "do" system of melodic syllables. Other counting and melodic reading methods may be used, if you wish, but the key is consistency and regular practice.

While the essence of this method is to avoid overloading the student with a lot of musical vocabulary and labels, the teacher is encouraged to be flexible and answer the questions that arise, even if it means jumping ahead briefly. These "teachable moments" will surely save time in the long run.

How To Use This Book

THE CHORAL APPROACH TO SIGHT-SINGING can be part of a successful sight-singing program if you will consider several basic principles:

1. Boys are intelligent and willing, and they can be the foundation of a successful choir. They can and will learn to sight-read quickly and well.

2. Rhythm accounts for more than 50% of the difficulty in sight-reading, so this method separates the concepts of rhythm and pitch. Always emphasize and reinforce rhythmic comprehension. Go beyond understanding to habit.

3. Young male and female singers need to be equally fluent in treble and bass clef notation in order to be aware of how their part relates to the whole. Encourage them to read the clefs interchangeably in the combinable exercises (in their own register). It will be more appropriate to stay within their own parts on actual songs.

4. The comprehensive teaching suggestions, lesson plans, and other helpful hints which are included in the Teacher's Edition are based on an "average" situation. Differences in age, maturity, sophistication, as well as ethnic and regional differences will necessitate adjustments. Teachers are encouraged to adapt as necessary for their own individual situations.

5. Limit the time for sight-reading, even if the students are successful and feeling extra confident. 10-15 minutes daily should usually be sufficient.

6. Remember the value of repetition. Go back and review previously covered material for extra reinforcement and confidence building.

7. Try to keep all students involved at all times, either by studying or practicing their own part silently, or by singing each other's part. Remember, if you don't find things for them to do with their minds and mouths, they will!

8. Always be musical, whether working with songs or exercises.

9. Stress to the students, that you will do everything in your power to not waste their time, and expect the same in return.

10. In learning your "other" music for concert performance, help students to transfer their sight-singing skills to other situations. In addition, supplement this method with songs that the students are able to sight-read all or portions of.

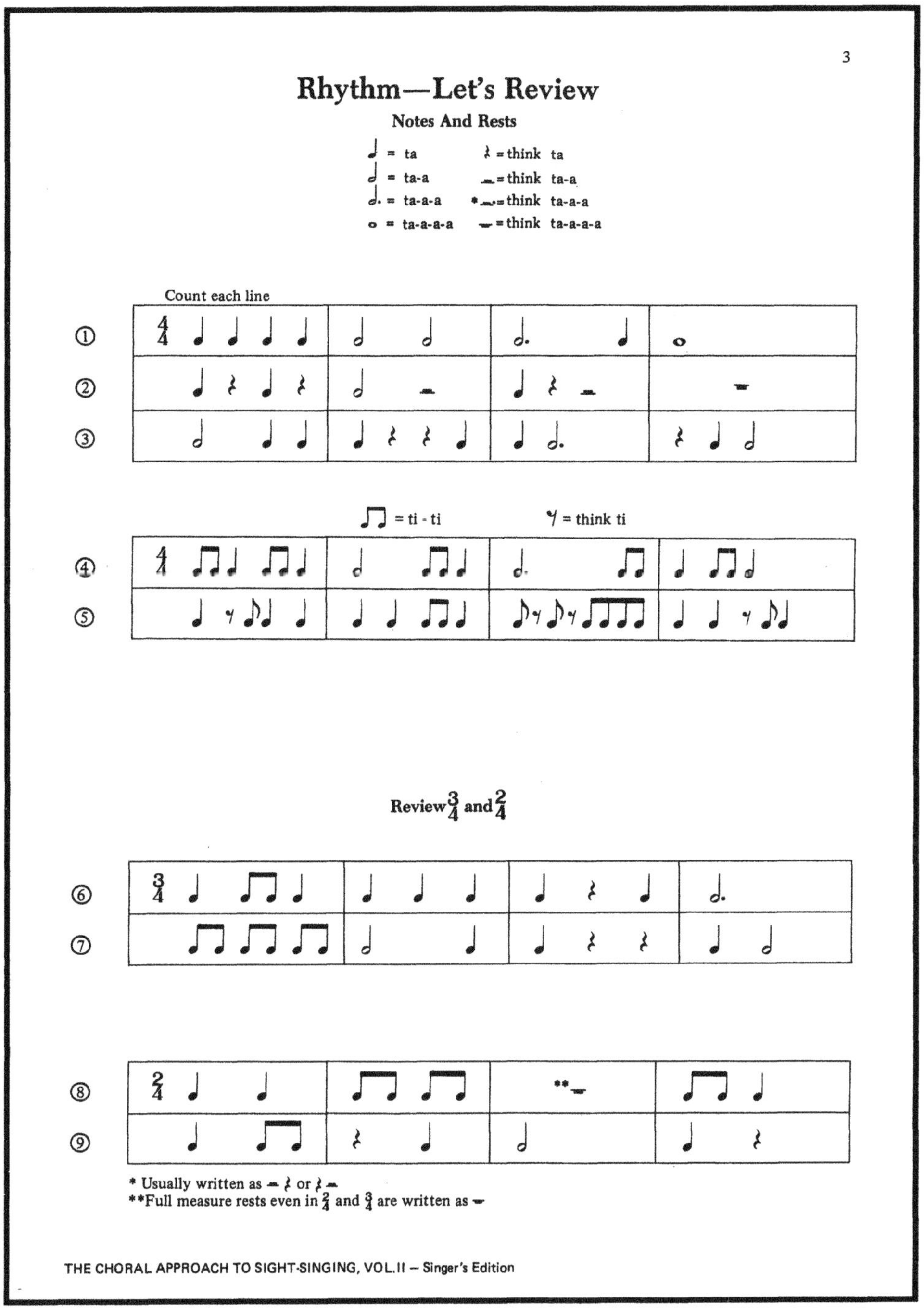
3

Rhythm—Let's Review

Notes And Rests

♩ = ta — 𝄽 = think ta
𝅗𝅥 = ta-a — = think ta-a
𝅗𝅥. = ta-a-a — * = think ta-a-a
𝅝 = ta-a-a-a — = think ta-a-a-a

Count each line

①
②
③

= ti - ti — = think ti

④
⑤

Review 3/4 and 2/4

⑥
⑦

⑧
⑨

* Usually written as 𝄼 𝄽 or 𝄽 𝄼
**Full measure rests even in 2/4 and 3/4 are written as 𝄻

THE CHORAL APPROACH TO SIGHT-SINGING, VOL.II – Singer's Edition

Rhythm — Let's Review

Teaching Suggestions:

Concepts:

- Review notes and their corresponding rests.

- Review the steady beat.
- Review 4/4, 3/4, and 2/4, and the unspoken concept of measure and phrase.

Directions:

- Count each line. Keep a uniform tempo. Gauge the tempo according to the most difficult measure. The tempo may increase as the students gain facility and confidence with the various combinations of notes and rests.
- Count each group of 4/4 exercises without stopping.
- Count each group of 3/4 exercises without stopping.
- Count each group of 2/4 exercises without stopping.
- Make up your own combinations.
- If these exercises seem overly difficult, go back to Vol. I for a few reminder sessions.
- Compare the exercises to reinforce the difference between the three meters.

NOTE: While other counting methods may be adapted to work with this material, the syllable "ta" was chosen for uniformity.

♩ is "ta" regardless of its position in the measure.

Key Of F — Review And Practice

Teaching Suggestions:

Concepts:

- Key of F
- Treble Clef and Bass Clef

- Harmony (Chord progressions)

Directions:

- Sing the scale and call attention to the fact that the notes sound in unison, despite being written in different clefs. The singers may omit the notes that are out of their range. Remember that the whole 3-Part Mixed concept is based on the lower part being a "compromise range", so some of your singers may not be able to sing all of the notes all of the time. Encourage them to sing the notes that they can, and sing mentally the notes that are out of their range.
- Review the treble and bass clefs briefly, so that the singers can locate their own staff. Point out that the bracket joining the staves on the left means that the lines are sung concurrently.
- Sing a pitch ladder (tonic chord). This will give structure to the key feeling and will help the singers find their starting pitch.
- Sing the chord drill. This will help the singers with blend, balance, tuning, following the director, and listening to the entire ensemble. At this point, it may be better to avoid using lots of technical terms (dominant, sub-dominant, etc.). Concentrate on the location of <u>do</u> as the key center, and the relationship of the other notes to <u>do</u>.
- On each exercise, count each line using rhythm syllables, sing each line in solfege, then sing parts together.
- Allow the parts to interchange occasionally, to be sure that everyone understand the relationships of the respective parts.

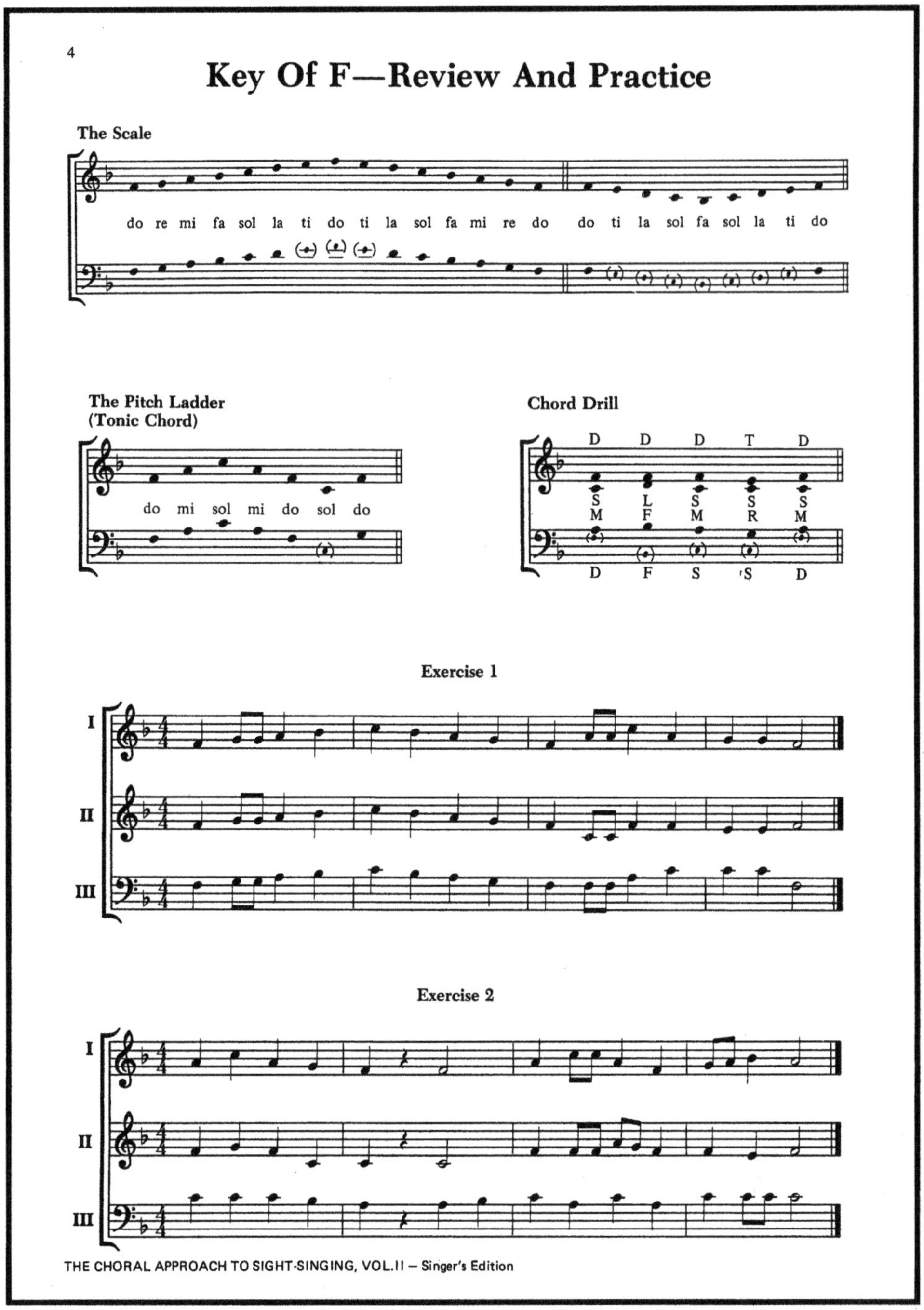

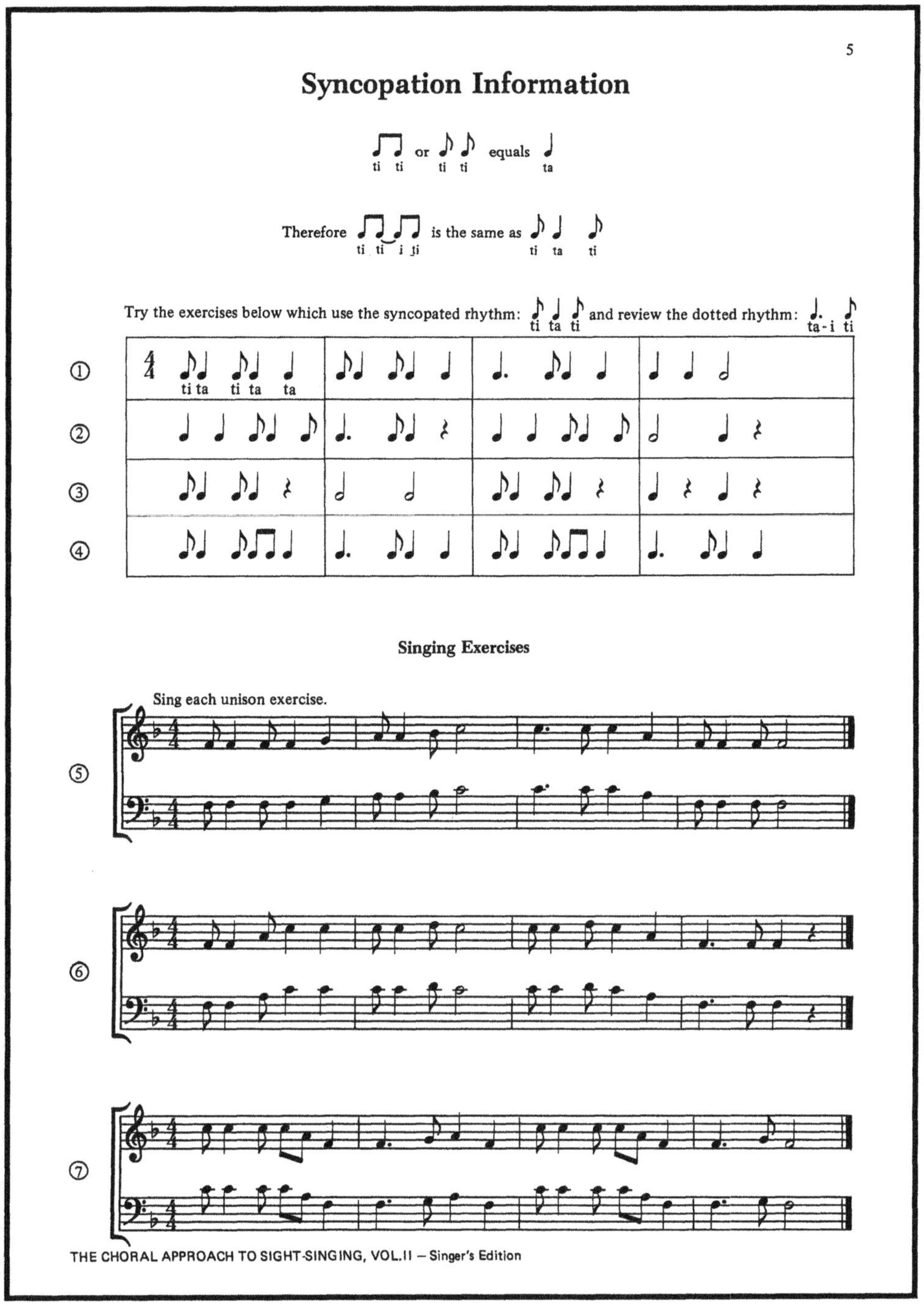

Syncopation Information

Teaching Suggestions:

Concepts:

- Introduce syncopation

- Practice rhythm patterns and rests
- Review dotted rhythms

- Treble voices on one line and lower voices on one line in unison to reinforce the relationship of the two clefs

Directions:

- Read and discuss the explanation of syncopation in the student book.
- Keeping a steady beat, count the rhythm exercises, repeating as needed. Review dotted rhythms in Volume I if necessary.
- If the concept of syncopation seems confusing, demonstrate it by rote and/or sing some examples of songs which use syncopation (Li'l Liza Jane, Our Boys Will Shine Tonight, etc.). Once they hear it and see it, it will be more easily understood.
- On lines 5-7, count the rhythm, then sing each line in solfege.
- Play "Catch Me" by having one person start to sing, and as they locate the line being sung, join in.

More Practice With Syncopation

Teaching Suggestions:

Concepts:

- Practice Syncopation
- Develop vocal independence
- Repetition without boredom
- Sharpen sight-reading skills
- Greater familiarity with bass and treble clefs
- The importance of "keep moving" even after making a mistake. The repetition of patterns will build confidence.

Directions:

- Count the first two lines to reinforce the new rhythm.
- Try counting the whole page without stopping. There may be a stumble or two, especially with the dotted patterns, but try to keep going.
- The last line is the most difficult. It may be necessary to practice the rhythm several times before moving on to pitch.
- Sing the lines in solfege, in unison if possible, or as close as the boys' range will allow.
- Sing the lines in any combination, then switch lines and try other combinations.

NOTE: Since this page is designed to build confidence, this is a good place to start dividing into more parts.

Remember that the 3rd and 7th scale degrees ("mi" and "ti") have a natural tendency to go flat. Be especially careful when "mi" is the final note of a long phrase.

6

More Practice With Syncopation

Sing each exercise separately or in any combination.

Higher Voices

① ② ③ ④ ⑤ ⑥

Lower Voices

⑦ ⑧ ⑨

THE CHORAL APPROACH TO SIGHT-SINGING, VOL.II – Singer's Edition

Two Songs

Teaching Suggestions:

Concepts:

- Practice syncopation
- Song with lyrics
- Review "two-line" songs (The song isn't over until you reach the double bar!) and the concept of bracketed three-staff systems.

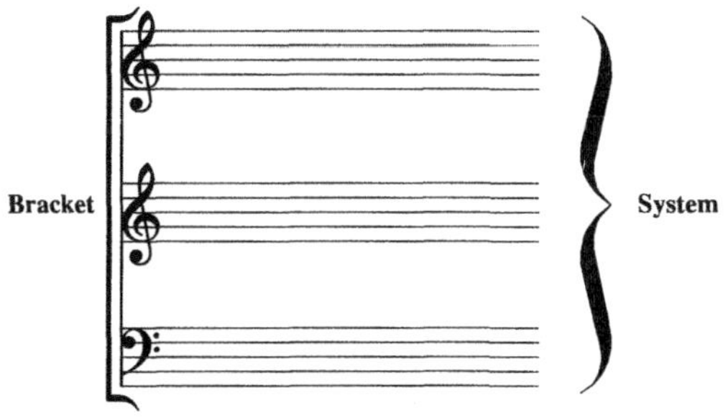

- Optional cue-sized notes for those boys with changed voices.

Directions:

LIZA JANE

- Count the rhythm.
- Sing Part I in solfege.
- Sing Parts II and III in solfege or on a neutral syllable.
- Sing a tonic chord to establish the pitch, then sing through in solfege.
- Add lyrics; repeat as needed.

OUR TEAM WILL WIN!
HELLO!

- Count the rhythm
- Sing in solfege or on a neutral syllable.
- Add lyrics; sing as a round.
- Encourage any changed voices to use the optional cue-sized notes.

NOTE: The sequence of preparation and amount of repetition necessary for optimum success will vary.

Key Of G — Review And Practice

Teaching Suggestions:

Concepts:

- Review the key of G scale, tonic chord, and chord drill.
- Review the most common meter signatures: 4/4, 3/4, and 2/4.
- Practice good blend, balance, and intonation.

Directions:

- Point out the new location of <u>do</u> and sing the scale. Repeat.
- Sing the tonic chord (pitch ladder).
- Sing the chord drill, giving special attention to pitch, blend, and choral balance. Always sing musically, even on exercises.
- Devise your own variations on the chord drill to sharpen pitch awareness. Remember to avoid flatting on <u>mi</u> and <u>ti</u>.
- Compare the meter signatures on the three exercises.
- On each exercise, let the singers count their own part mentally, establish the starting pitch with a tonic chord, then sing in solfege.
- Repeat immediately, allowing them to correct their own errors. Make corrections only after they have failed to make their own corrections on two or more efforts.

NOTE: It may be necessary to isolate the following patterns:
1) In "Sometimes In 2/4", you may need to isolate the dotted patterns in Part II.
2) In "Usually in 4/4", do a spot review of the intervals <u>fa</u>-<u>re</u> and <u>re</u>-<u>ti</u>.

See if the singers can mentally shift gears and sing through all the exercises without a stop.

Exercises In G

Teaching Suggestions:

Concepts:

- More practice with 8 measure exercises.
- Key of G review.
- Practice reading rests, especially the eighth rest (ti).
- The confusing, but common practice of using a whole rest even when there are not four beats in a measure. It automatically stands for the number of beats in the meter signature.

Directions:

NAME THAT TUNE (Skip To My Lou)

- Mentally review the rhythm and pitch to see if the students can identify the song without saying the title aloud.
- Sing a tonic chord, tune the starting pitches, and sing in solfege. The students can raise their hands as they recognize the song, but they should keep singing. Repeat as needed.
- Note the slur and optional divisi at the end of part III.
- Can they add lyrics?

REST (BUT DON'T RELAX)

- In advance, isolate the eighth rest (ti), the quarter rest, and the whole rest, and review how they are to be counted.
- Count the rhythm. Watch out for tricky spots!
- Sing the exercises in solfege. Don't sing on the rests! Repeat as needed.
- Help the students become conscious of rests in their choral repertoire.

"This Train"

Teaching Suggestions:

Concepts:

- Syncopation.

- Review ties.
- Interval skips in the I, IV, and V chords.
- Dynamics — especially the concept of sudden dynamic changes (subito p in m. 22).
- Augmentation.

Directions:

- Count the rhythm, noticing the place where Part I has a different rhythm.
- Speak the solfege in rhythm, noticing difficult intervals (<u>fa</u>-<u>re</u>, <u>do</u>-<u>la</u>, etc.). Isolate the difficult intervals before singing.
- Establish the starting pitch. Refer to the chord drill on p. 8 for more pitch security, and sing through in solfege. Repeat as needed to correct errors.
- Add the accompaniment.
- Add the words.
- Find the place that uses rhythmic augmentation (same notes — twice as long).
- Sing through with all dynamics.

11
This train is bound for glo-ry, all who ride it must be ho-ly. This train is bound for glo-ry,
This train is bound for glo-ry, all who ride it must be ho-ly. This train is bound for glo-ry,
This train is bound for glo-ry, all who ride it must be ho-ly. This train is bound for glo-ry,
mp
11
this train... We'll soon be done with toil and trial, we'll walk with the Lord a-while. We'll
this train... We're done with trou-ble, we're done with trial. We'll
this train... We're done with trou-ble, we're done with trial. We'll
THE CHORAL APPROACH TO SIGHT-SINGING, VOL.II – Singer's Edition

NOTES

NOTES

12
sit down at the wel-come ta-ble, climb a-board now if you're a-ble. This train is bound for glo-ry,
sit at the ta-ble, so climb a-board now if you're a-ble. This train is bound for glo-ry,
sit at the ta-ble, so climb a-board now if you're a-ble. This train is bound for glo-ry,
this train.__ This train is bound for glo-ry, this train.__
this train.__ This train is bound for glo-ry, this train.__
this train.__ This train is bound for glo-ry, this train.__
THE CHORAL APPROACH TO SIGHT-SINGING, VOL.II – Singer's Edition

13
This train is bound for glo-ry, all who ride it must be ho-ly. This train is bound for glo-ry,
This train is bound for glo-ry, all who ride it must be ho-ly. This train is bound for glo-ry,
This train is bound for glo-ry, all who ride it must be ho-ly. This train is bound for glo-ry,
sub p
f
all who ride it must be ho-ly. This train is bound for glo - ry, this train.
sub p
f
all who ride it must be ho-ly. This train is bound for glo - ry, this train.
sub p
f
all who ride it must be ho-ly. This train is bound for glo - ry, this train.
sub p
f
THE CHORAL APPROACH TO SIGHT-SINGING, VOL.II – Singer's Edition

NOTES

Key Of D — Review And Practice

Teaching Suggestions:

Concepts:

- Review the key of D scale, tonic chord, and chord drill.
- Review how to find <u>do</u> (Refer to Vol. I, p. 58, if necessary.)
- Practice blend, balance, and intonation.
- Optional 4th (bass) part for changed voices.
- Uncommon and very challenging intervals, and extended vocal ranges.

Directions:

- Point out the new location of <u>do</u> and sing the scale. Repeat.
- Sing the tonic chord (pitch ladder).
- Sing the chord drill, giving special attention to pitch, balance, and blend. If possible, divide the male voices by having the changed voices sing the cue sized lower notes.

CLASSIC MELODY ("To A Wild Rose") by MacDowell)

- Parts II and III are easy, but the melody, Part I is loaded with uncommon intervals. Warn the students that this melody is more challenging than most, and give extra practice time before starting to sing.
- Have all the singers sight-read Part I in unison. Say the syllables in solfege, perhaps twice, before singing them.
- Establish the starting pitch and sing in solfege. Repeat as necessary.
- Divide into parts and sing in harmony. Note the new lower notes for Part II.
- Can you improvise a piano part?

15

Challenge!

Learn to look ahead for unexpected challenges and prepare for them in advance. Locate these spots in "Two Wings" and be ready for them. Are there others?

3-Note Pick-up

Octave Leap

do do la sol

Syncopation

Two Wings

(♩ = 108)

Spiritual

I, II, III

Oh, Lord, I want two wings to hide my face. Oh Lord, I want two wings to fly a-way. Oh Lord, I want two wings to hide my face, so the dev-il can't do me no harm.

THE CHORAL APPROACH TO SIGHT-SINGING, VOL. II – Singer's Edition

Challenge!

Teaching Suggestions:

Concepts:

- Key of D practice.
- 3-note pick-up:

- Octave leap in Part I:

- Syncopation using a rest:

- Sections which are alike or very similar.

Directions:

- Carefully read the instructions at the top of the student page, and locate those examples in advance. Demonstrate, if necessary.
- Count the rhythm at a slow tempo. What sections are alike or almost alike?
- Sing it slowly in solfege. Repeat.
- Sing it at the tempo given.
- Add lyrics.

Key Of A Flat — Review And Practice

Teaching Suggestions:

Concepts:

- Key of A flat review and practice.
- Practice blend, balance, and singing in tune.
- Review pick-up notes and 3/4 meter.

Directions:

- Practice finding do in A flat. (See Vol. I, p. 58, if necessary.)
- Review letter names of the lines and spaces, since the key name comes from the line or space where do is located.
- Sing the scale, tonic chord, and chord drill, pointing out the new notes. The students should sing as many of the new notes as possible. If any notes are out of their range, caution against over-extending the voice, or putting too much volume on "hard-to-reach" notes. Always be musical!

NAME THAT TUNE
("We Wish You A Merry Christmas")

- Establish the location of do (the key center) and sol (the starting pitch), the meter (3/4), and then give the singers approximately 30 seconds to study Part I and mentally try to identify the song.
- Sing the starting pitch, and sing Part I in solfege in unison. They can raise their hands when they recognize the tune.
- Sing all three parts in solfege.
- Add the words.

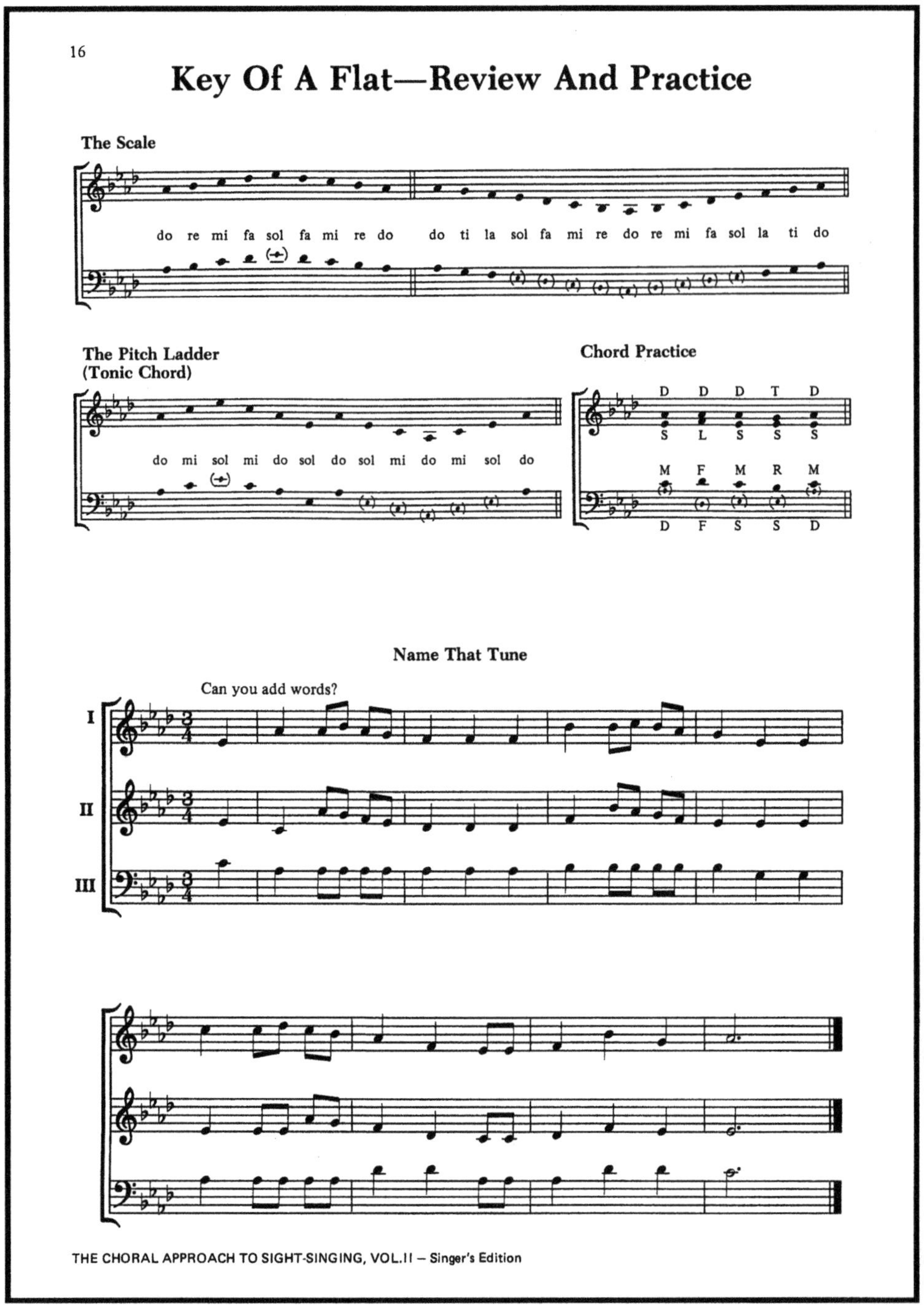

Can't Pick Bananas On Sunday

Teaching Suggestions:

Concepts:

- Review Key of A Flat
- Reinforce the difference between ties and slurs. (Ties connect notes of the same pitch, slurs connect notes of different pitches.)
- Review tied and dotted note patterns.

- Develop vocal independence by combining lines to produce harmony.
- Repetition of rhythm patterns develops sight-reading confidence.
- Students can add the written percussion and have the opportunity to create and notate their own patterns.

Directions:

- Which lines have the same rhythm.
- Where are the ties? The slurs? What is the difference?
- Isolate the following rhythm patterns? Where is it found on the page?

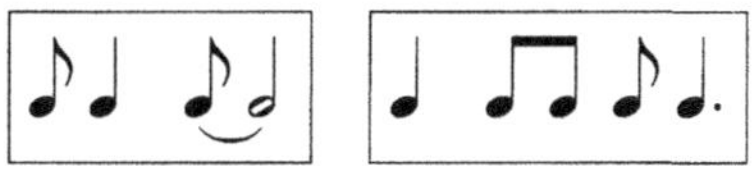

- Count the rhythm of each line.
- Sing all the lines in solfege, straight through, if possible (bass and treble clefs).
- Combine the lines for harmony.
- Count the rhythm of the percussion lines, and see how they are notated. Add percussion instruments. NOTE: The following pattern means "drum roll" or "shaken tambourine."

- Encourage the singers to create their own percussion patterns, and see if they can notate their efforts.

NOTE: Don't try to do all of these suggestions on a single day, even if the singers are performing well. The amount of repetition is designed to build confidence, but doing too much at one time could spoil the effect.

Key Of E Flat — Review And Practice

Teaching Suggestions:

Concepts:

- Key of E flat review.
- New notes and expanded vocal ranges.
- Practice finding do in a flat key.
- Trying to write words to fit an existing rhythm pattern helps develop an understanding of the function of rhythm and how it is notated.

Directions:

- Review how to find do.
- Sing the scale and tonic chord, pointing out the new notes that may be out of range for some. Sing as many of the notes as possible, but don't overextend the voice.
- Sing the chord drill, giving special attention to the lower voices. If at all possible, divide into two parts, having the changed voices sing the cue-size notes.

THREE PART PRACTICE

- Count the rhythm silently.
- Establish do, find the starting pitches and give the students 30 seconds to mentally sing their part.
- Sing the parts in solfege or on a neutral syllable, being careful to sing in tune, especially on mi and ti.
- Can the singers write their own words for the song? What subject does the music suggest? What needs to be changed and why? Experiment with changing the words to match the rhythm and with changing the rhythm to match the words.
- Note how syllable emphasis affects the rhythm, and vice versa.
- Encourage the students to try to notate other simple melodic or rhythm fragments, either familiar tunes or original patterns.

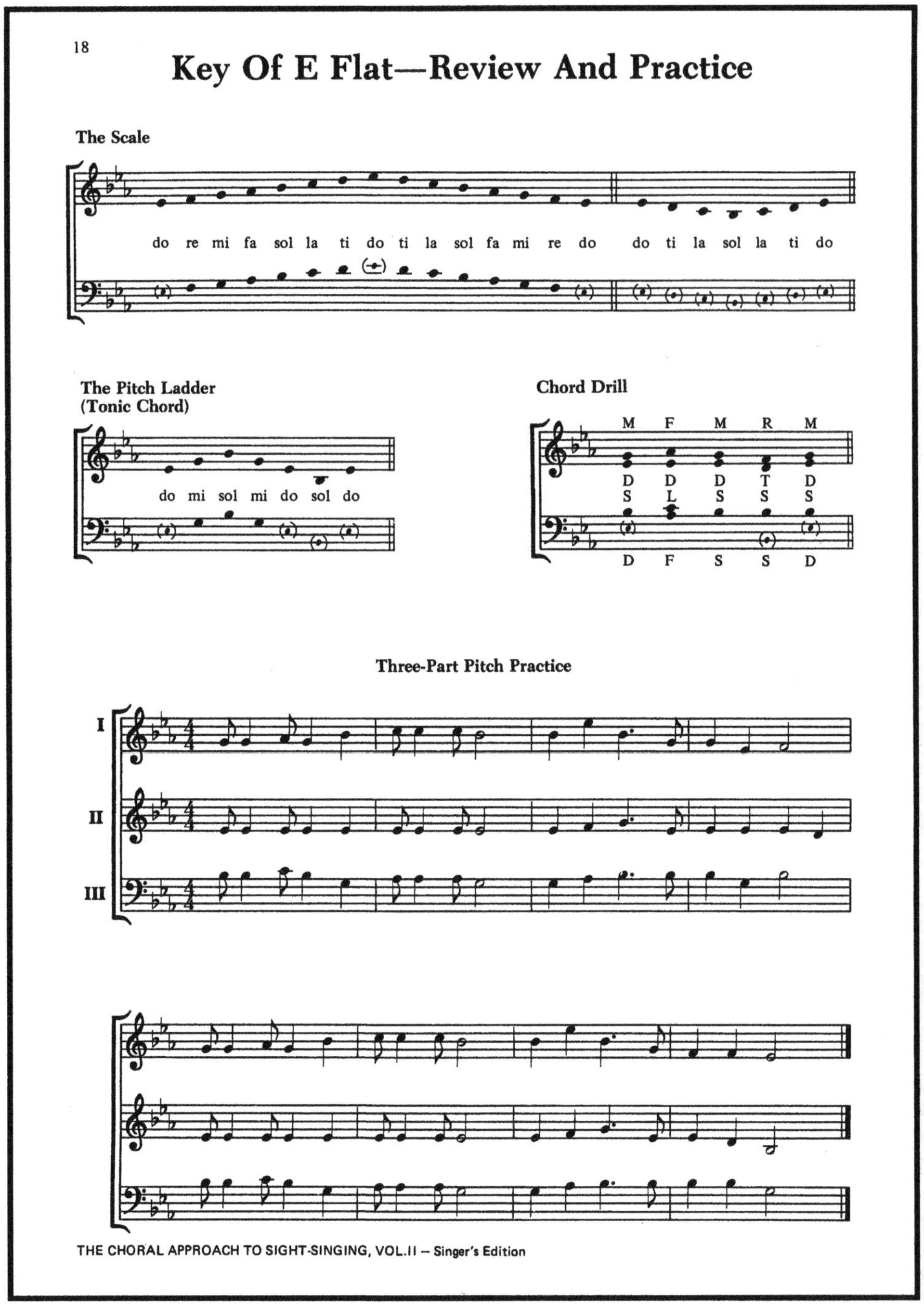

3/4 Singing Exercises — Key Of E Flat

Teaching Suggestions:

Concepts:

- Practice Key of E flat.
- Practice 3/4.
- Practice sight-reading 8-measure exercises.
- Practice looking ahead for what is coming up while singing. This is the real essence of musical literacy, and combinable exercises at this level of difficulty help the singers to develop this essential skill.

Directions:

- Establish <u>do</u> and look ahead to the starting pitch of each exercise.
- Try several options, depending on the facility of the particular group:

  1) Sing all the lines straight through in unison.

  2) Have each part select an exercise, establish the starting pitch, and go!

  3) Let each student select any exercise they like. Establish the starting pitches and begin singing. When you finish one line, skip to another. How long can they keep going?

NOTE: It is all right for the singers to switch between treble and bass clef, if they can handle the range and avoid straining the voice. The goal is to become fluent in both clefs.

OPTIONAL: Try writing lyrics for some of the exercises.

As with anything, don't overdo a good thing. Work long enough to benefit from the repetition, but not so long as to become bored after accomplishing the desired goals.

New Patterns — Sixteenth Notes

Teaching Suggestions:

Concepts:

- Introduce sixteenth notes and their various combinations.

ti ki ti ki   ti ti ki   ti ki ti

- Though usually beamed together, sixteenth notes may also be notated with flags.

ti ki ti ki   ti ki ti ki

Directions:

- Compare the examples in the singer's book, and demonstrate how sixteenth notes are counted.
- Study the first four lines for 15-30 seconds, establish a steady beat and read through the exercises in rhythm. Repeat as needed.
- Demonstrate and practice the following patterns:

ti ti ki ti ki ti

- Locate these patterns in exercises 5-8, then establish the steady beat and go! Repeat as needed.
- Play "Catch Me" by having one person start to count any line while the others join in as soon as they locate the right place.

NOTE: Don't rush. Gauge the tempo by the comfortable speed of the most active measure.

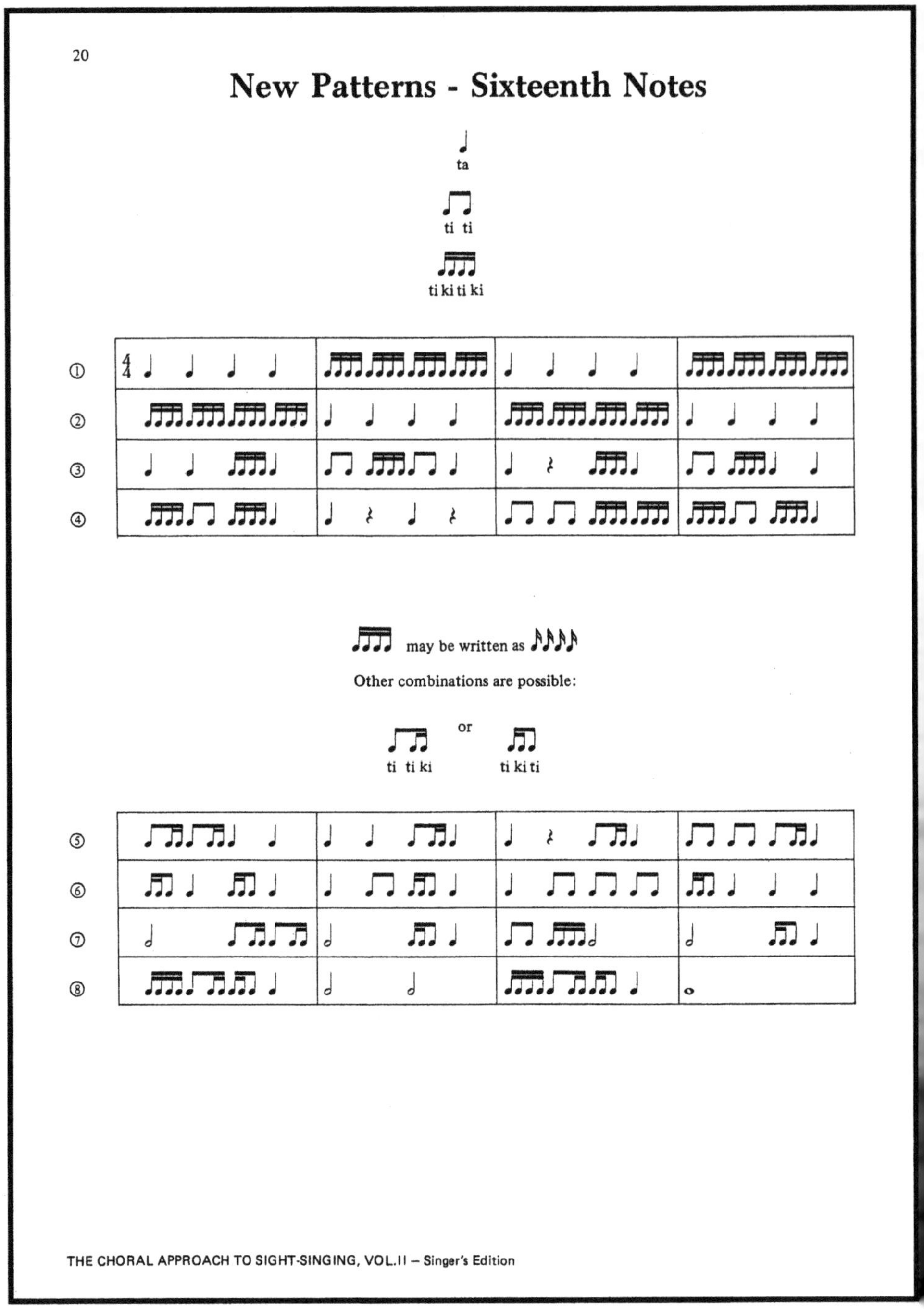

20

New Patterns - Sixteenth Notes

ta

ti ti

ti ki ti ki

may be written as

Other combinations are possible:

ti ti ki   or   ti ki ti

THE CHORAL APPROACH TO SIGHT-SINGING, VOL.II – Singer's Edition

Sixteenth Note Practice

Teaching Suggestions:

Concepts:

- Practice sixteenth note patterns.

- Review 2/4 and eighth rests.
- Practice finding <u>do</u> in a key with no sharps or flats. (<u>Do</u> is automatically "C")
- Sixteenth note pick-up.

- Accent: 

Directions:

- Review finding <u>do</u> in the keys of F and C.
- If needed, count each line separately, then establish the starting pitch and sing through in solfege. If the group is sufficiently capable, give them 30-60 seconds to study, then begin. Repeat as needed.
- Encourage the students to figure out the function of an accent through its use in context.

NAME THAT TUNE ("William Tell Overture" or "The Lone Ranger Theme")

- Allow the students to study mentally, then sight-read using the established sequence.

There Was An Old Man

Teaching Suggestions:

Concepts:

• Review sixteenth note patterns:

• 3-Part Practice in the key of C

• 16 measure a cappella song.

Directions:

• Establish do and sing the starting pitches, and silently review the rhythm and melody. Keep the tempo slow, but steady, and sing through with the text. (Be brave!) The sixteenth notes make it look harder than it actually is. The melody is mostly stepwise or easy intervals, so this can be a confidence builder. Don't rush!

• Keep going! Don't worry about minor mistakes — they can be corrected the second time through.

• Without verbal correction, give pitches and repeat the song. The singers will correct a vast majority of their errors the second time through.

REMEMBER: You must have the freedom to fail before you gain the courage to succeed.

• Additional verses are listed below. (NOTE: The rhythm must be adjusted to the new lyrics.)

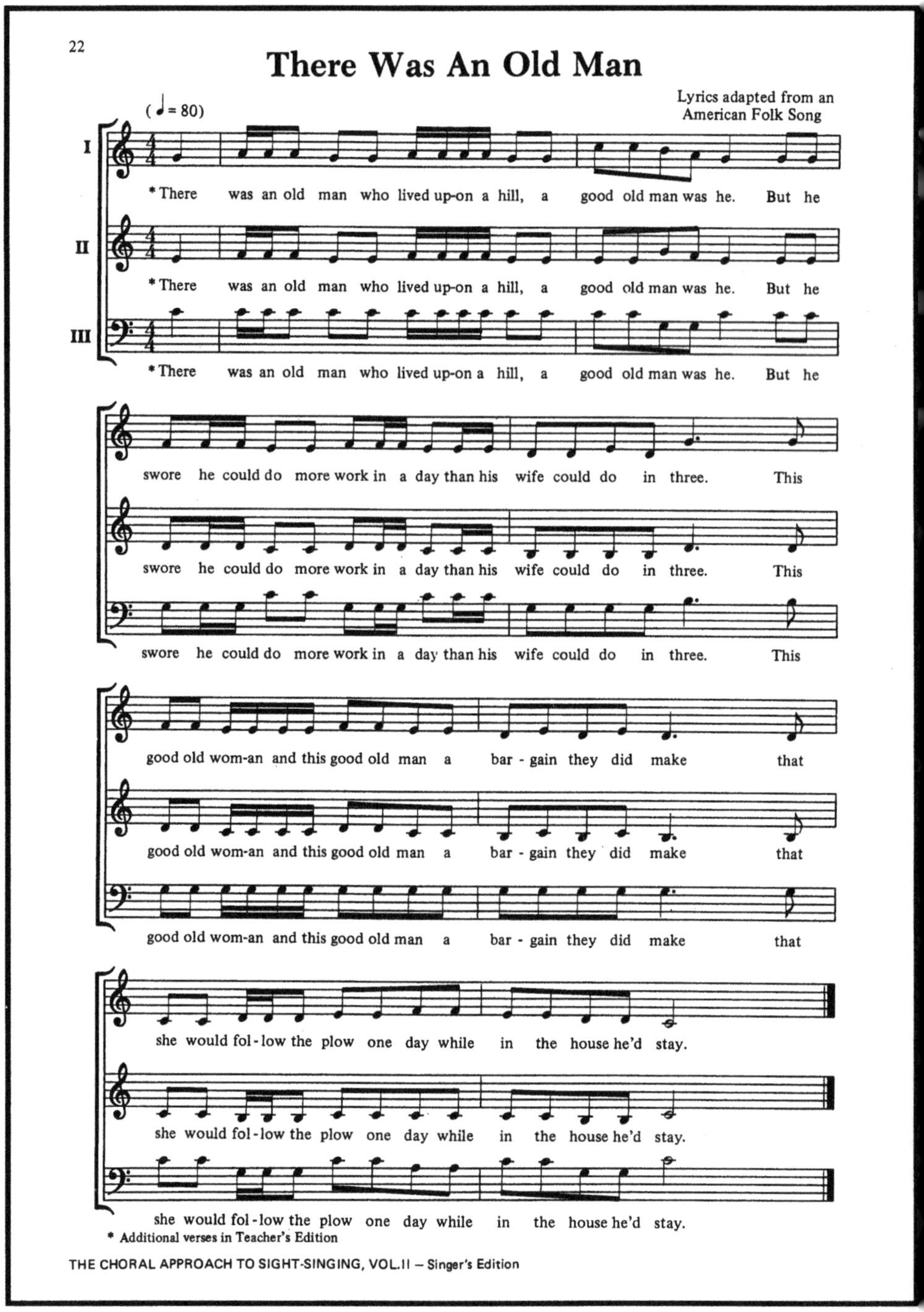

Verse 2:
"With all my heart," the old woman said, "If that you will allow.
Tomorrow you stay at home in my stead, and I'll go drive the plow."

Verse 3:
The old woman took the staff in her hand and went to drive the plow.
The old man took the pail in his hand and went to milk the cow.

Verse 4:
But the old cow hinched and the old cow flinched and the old cow broke his nose.
And the old cow gave him quite a blow and stepped all over his toes.

Verse 5:
He went to feed the little pigs that were within the sty.
He hit his head against the beam and blackened both his eyes.

Verse 6:
So he cried to the sun and the moon and the stars and the green leaves on the tree,
'Tis true, she can do more work in a day than I can do in three.

Gloria

Teaching Suggestions:

Concepts:

- Key of F practice.
- Sixteenth note review.
- Practice with slurs and ties.
- Crescendo and descrescendo

- Work on breath support, vowel purity and Latin pronunciation.
- An "easy-to-sight-read" fragment that can show the students how far they have come, and build confidence for more challenge in the future. Singers should be encouraged to be aware of more than just the rhythms and pitches.

Directions:

- Establish do and the starting pitches.
- Study silently for 15-30 seconds, looking especially for potential problems.
- Re-establish starting pitches and GO! Because it starts in unison, the singers may become over-confident and miss the split into harmony in m. 5. Insist that they keep going, and they will probably do better the next time.
- After silently taking time to locate and review mistakes, repeat.
- Point out and briefly discuss the dynamics.
- Review slurs and ties, their functions, differences, and locations. Note the long slurs and the effect they have on the amount of breath that is needed. The singers must become conscious of all these additional elements anytime they are sight-reading.
- Repeat, singing as musically as possible, and trying to use all the musical elements correctly.

Rhythm Review and New Patterns

Teaching Suggestions:

Concepts:

- Review the rule for reading tied rhythms: Drop the "ti" from the note that is tied.

For a more extensive review, refer to Vol. I.

- Introduce new sixteenth note patterns:

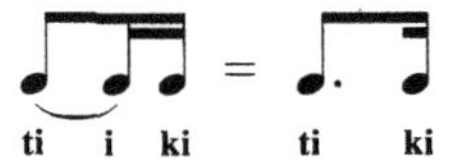

Directions:

- Review the rule for reading tied notes.
- Discuss the examples and find them in lines 1-4. Find ties in lines 1-4 not covered by the examples and use the rule to figure out how to count them.
- Introduce the new dotted eighth/sixteenth pattern, read, discuss, and demonstrate the examples in the student book.
- If the students seem confused, don't hesitate to demonstrate further, using song fragments from familiar tunes: "Star-Spangled Banner," "Down At The Station," etc.
- Count lines 5-8. Repeat.

NOTE: This page might prove to be difficult the first time it is attempted, so divide it over several lessons. In the future, come back and review this page and see how easy it seems.

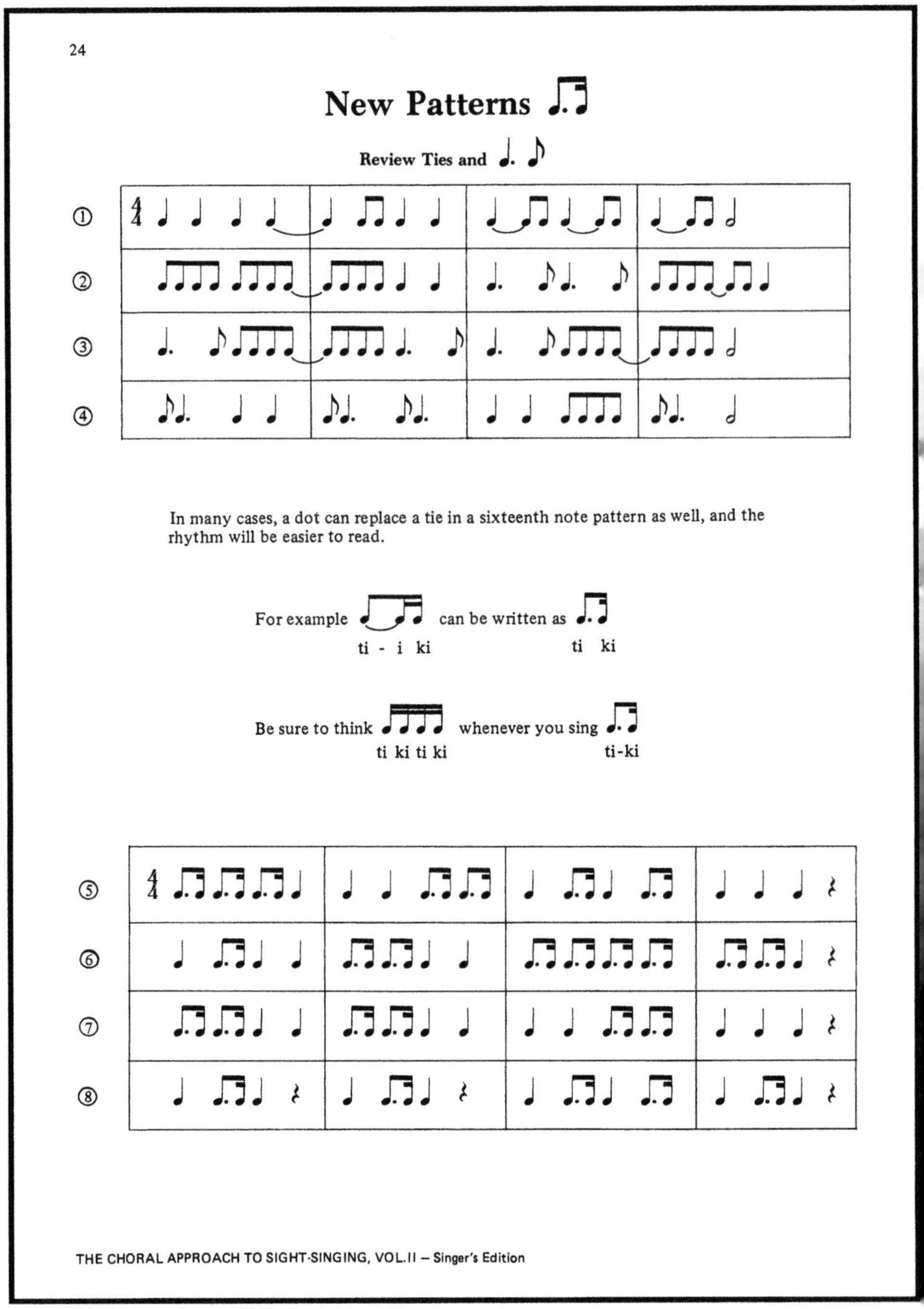
24

New Patterns

Review Ties and

① ② ③ ④

In many cases, a dot can replace a tie in a sixteenth note pattern as well, and the rhythm will be easier to read.

For example can be written as
ti - i ki   ti ki

Be sure to think whenever you sing
ti ki ti ki   ti-ki

⑤ ⑥ ⑦ ⑧

THE CHORAL APPROACH TO SIGHT-SINGING, VOL. II – Singer's Edition

Three-Part Practice — Key Of F

Teaching Suggestions:

Concepts:

- Practice new rhythm pattern:

- Review 3/4 meter.
- Continue to develop melodic and rhythmic independence.
- Review slurs.

Directions:

- For both songs, read the rhythm silently and aloud noticing the places where the voices do not have the same rhythm.
- Concentrate on performing the dotted eighth/sixteenth pattern accurately.

- In "Song In 3/4" notice how the dotted pattern passes from voice to voice. Encourage the singers to emphasize this pattern, singing slightly louder whenever it occurs in their part.
- Speak the pitch syllables in rhythm silently and aloud.
- Establish the starting pitches and sing through in solfege. Repeat to correct mistakes.
- For "Joyfully Sing!" repeat once more with the text.

Key Of B Flat — Review And Practice

Teaching Suggestions:

Concepts:

- Review and practice key of B flat.
- Practice dynamics:

p

mp

mf

f

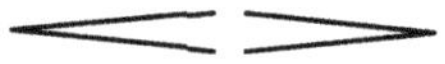

(For definitions, refer to Glossary)

- Practice dotted eighth/sixteenth rhythm pattern:

- Identifying sections that are alike or almost alike.

Directions:

- Sing the scale, tonic chord, and chord drill, using previously established procedures.
- Review the dynamics, discuss their function, and locate them in the song.
- Scan through the song to identify sections that are alike or nearly alike.
- If necessary, count the rhythm silently or aloud.
- Establish do and the starting pitches and then sing, using solfege or a neutral syllable.
- Review and repeat, this time with dynamics.
- Add the text.

NOTE: Emphasize the importance of performing the dotted pattern accurately.

27
loosed the fate-ful light-ning of His ter-ri-ble swift sword. His truth is march-ing
loosed the fate-ful light-ning of His ter-ri-ble swift sword. His truth is march-ing
loosed the fate-ful light-ning of His ter-ri-ble swift sword. His truth is march-ing
9
p
on. Glo - ry, glo - ry, hal - le - lu - jah!
p
on. Glo - ry, glo - ry, hal - le - lu - jah!
p
on. Glo - ry, glo - ry, hal - le - lu - jah!
mp
mf
Glo - ry, glo - ry, hal - le - lu - jah! Glo - ry, glo - ry, hal - le -
mp
mf
Glo - ry, glo - ry, hal - le - lu - jah! Glo - ry, glo - ry, hal - le -
mp
mf
Glo - ry, glo - ry, hal - le - lu - jah! Glo - ry, glo - ry, hal - le -
f
lu - jah! His truth is march - ing on!
f
lu - jah! His truth is march - ing on!
f
lu - jah! His truth is march - ing on!
THE CHORAL APPROACH TO SIGHT-SINGING, VOL.II – Singer's Edition

NOTES:

"Wheel's A-Turnin'"

Teaching Suggestions:

Concepts:

- Sight-read a song that incorporates several rhythm patterns that are slightly different, stressing rhythmic accuracy.

- Review dynamics within the context of a song.
- Discover sections that are the same or almost the same.
- Develop vocal and rhythmic independence by singing a song in which the piano accompaniment does not directly duplicate the voices.

Directions:

- Review the following rhythm patterns, keeping a steady beat, and emphasizing rhythmic accuracy. Do not choose a tempo that is too fast.

- Read the voice parts aloud in rhythm, noticing the places where the voice parts do not have the same rhythm.
- Study the solfege silently and then speak the solfege syllables aloud in rhythm. Concentrate on rhythmic precision.
- Establish <u>do</u> and sing a cappella in solfege. Repeat as needed. Emphasize the importance of rhythmic accuracy.
- Add the accompaniment and sing in solfege or on a neutral syllable. Notice how the left hand of the piano provides a continual sixteenth note subdivision in measures 1-6, 11-14, and 19-22.
- Sing again, with text and dynamics.

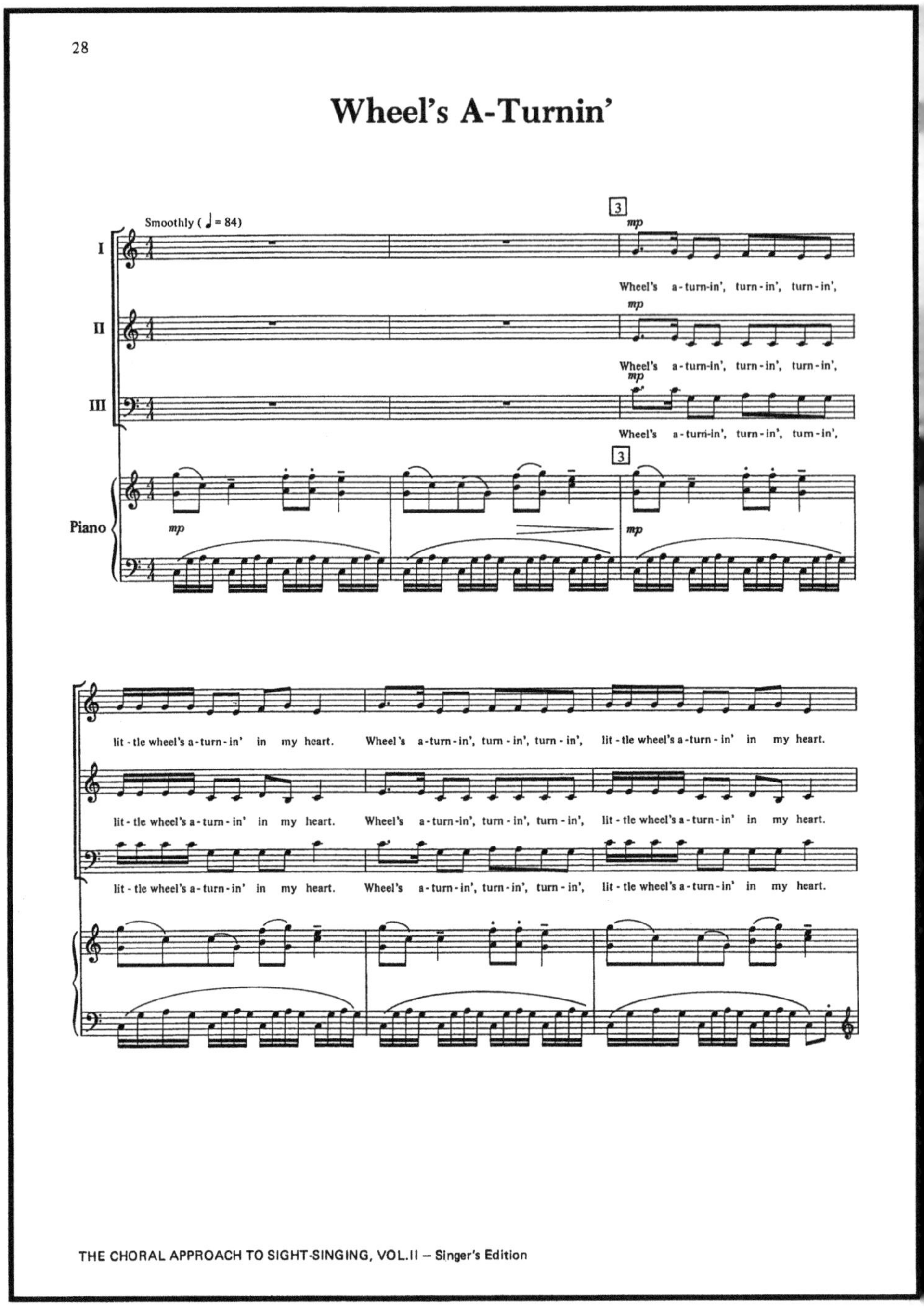

29

THE CHORAL APPROACH TO SIGHT-SINGING, VOL.II – Singer's Edition

NOTES:

NOTES:

30
15
Wheel's a - turn - in', turn - in', turn - in', lit - tle wheel's a - turn - in' in my heart.
Wheel's a - turn - in', turn - in', turn - in', lit - tle wheel's a - turn - in' in my heart.
f
Wheel's a - turn - in', turn - in', turn - in', lit - tle wheel's a - turn - in' in my heart. Where are the He - brew chil - dren?
15
f
f
Where are the He - brew chil - dren? Safe in the Prom - ised Land.
f
Where are the He - brew chil - dren? Safe in the Prom - ised Land.
Safe in the Prom - ised Land. Where are the He - brew chil - dren? Safe in the Prom - ised Land.
THE CHORAL APPROACH TO SIGHT-SINGING, VOL.II – Singer's Edition

31

THE CHORAL APPROACH TO SIGHT-SINGING, VOL. II – Singer's Edition

NOTES:

Counting In Six — 6/8

Teaching Suggestions:

Concepts:

- Introduce 6/8 meter — patterns based on ♪ instead of ♩
- More complex rhythms.

Directions:

- Read and discuss the explanation in the singer's edition.
- Look over lines 1-5 and remind the singers about the rule for reading tied rhythms (see p. 24). When reading tied rhythms, eliminate the consonant of the note that is tied.
- Read lines 1-5 — the students will learn more quickly by doing rather than discussing.
- Point out the difference in counting the note:

in 4/4 or 3/4 and 6/8.

ON YOUR OWN!

- Count lines 6-9. Repeat.
- Count lines 1-9 straight through without stopping.
- Refer to this page often before singing or rehearsing songs in 6/8.

6/8 Practice

Teaching Suggestions:

Concepts:

- 6/8 practice.
- Pick-up note in 6/8.
- Three part round.

Directions:

Find "Do" and Go!

- Count the rhythm.
- Sing in solfege. Repeat.

Lovely Evening

- Count the rhythm.
- Sing in solfege. Repeat.
- Add the lyrics.
- Sing it as a round.

NAME THAT TUNE ("I Saw Three Ships")

- Study the song silently to locate any potential problems.
- The song is in unison, except for m. 4 where the boys' part is altered to accommodate their limited range.
- Establish do and sing the starting pitch, establish the steady beat, and begin. (They should raise their hand when they recognize the tune.)
- Review the lyrics and sing again.

6/8 Notes And Rests

Teaching Suggestions:

Concepts:

- Practice 6/8 notes and their corresponding rests.

Directions:

- Compare 6/8 notes with their corresponding rests.
- Count lines 1-4.
- Repeat.
- Study lines 5-7 to locate any potential difficult spots.
- Count lines 5-7. Repeat.
- Count all lines without stopping.

NOTE: Avoid the temptation to rush the tempo in 6/8.

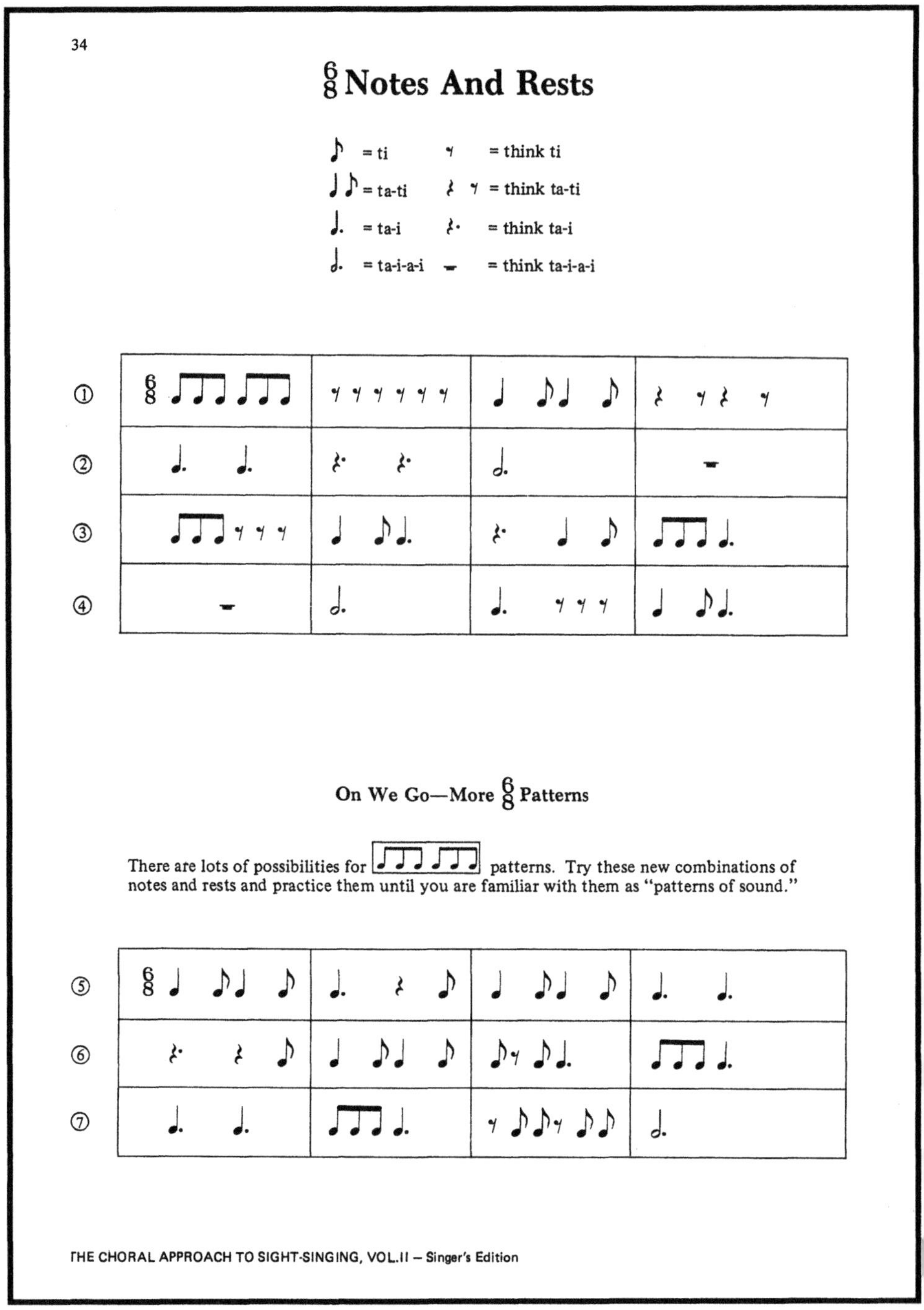

6/8 Combinations — Key Of D

Teaching Suggestions:

Concepts:

- More practice with 6/8 rhythms.
- Key of D practice.
- Melodic and rhythmic independence through combinable exercises and the resulting harmonic security.

Directions:

- Count each line and sing it in solfege.
- Repeat as needed.
- Sing the exercises separately and in any combination.
- Sing again, allowing each singer to choose their own line to develop confidence and vocal independence.

OLÉ

- Count the rhythm (including claps!)
- Sing in solfege. Repeat as needed.
- When the singers are familiar with this song, it can be an excellent chord drill.

Harvest Home

Teaching Suggestions:

Concepts:

- Accompanied song in 6/8, key of D.
- Addition of an optional 4th (bass) part.
- Skips within the I and IV chords.

Directions:

- Read through the rhythm silently, then aloud, concentrating on the places where the voices do not have the same rhythm.
- Speak the solfege syllables in rhythm, noting the spots where the tonic chord is outlined and other challenging intervals. (Watch out for m. 11 where there is a skip from do to fa.)
- Sing through a key of D chord drill to prepare for the harmony.
- Establish the starting pitches and sing through in solfege. Repeat as needed, isolating difficult spots, if necessary.
- Be sure to keep a steady beat. Don't rush!
- Sing again with the lyrics.
- Add the accompaniment.
- Sing again, up to tempo and with all dynamics.

37
Soon the fields are bright and green. The gold - en corn will
Soon the fields are bright and green. The gold - en corn will
Soon the fields are bright and green. The gold - en corn will
11
soon be seen. Now the work - ers' voic - es ring, of
soon be seen. Now the work - ers' voic - es ring, of
soon be seen. Now the work - ers' voic - es ring, of
11
THE CHORAL APPROACH TO SIGHT-SINGING, VOL.II – Singer's Edition

NOTES:

NOTES:

38
f
har - vest home they glad - ly sing. Har - vest home,
har - vest home they glad - ly sing. Har - vest home,
har - vest home they glad - ly sing. Har - vest home,
har - vest home, they glad - ly sing of their har - vest home.
har - vest home, they glad - ly sing of their har - vest home.
har - vest home, they glad - ly sing of their har - vest home.
THE CHORAL APPROACH TO SIGHT-SINGING, VOL.II – Singer's Edition

Accidentals

These three symbols are called accidentals and affect notes which follow them:

1. A sharp (♯♩) raises a pitch by a half step.
2. A flat (♭♩) lowers a pitch by a half step.
3. A natural (♮♩) cancels a previous sharp or flat.

Here is a chart for determining the pitch syllable for an altered note:

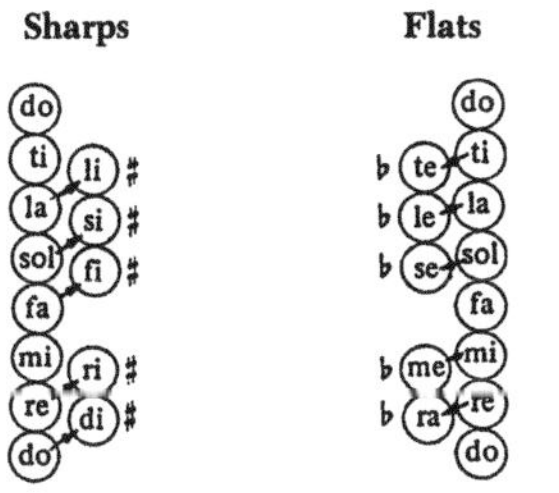

A chromatic scale is one which moves up or down by halfsteps.

Ascending Chromatic Scale

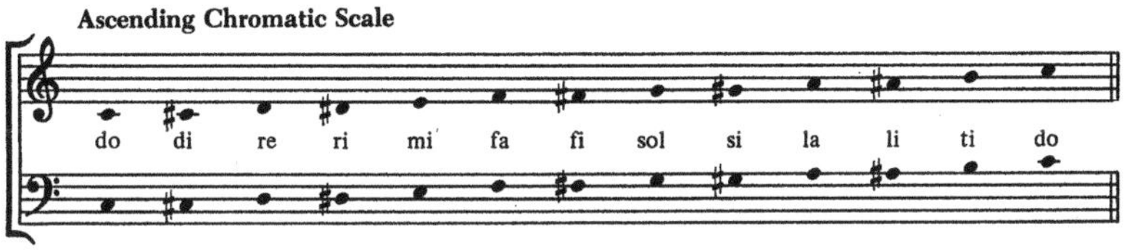

Descending Chromatic Scale

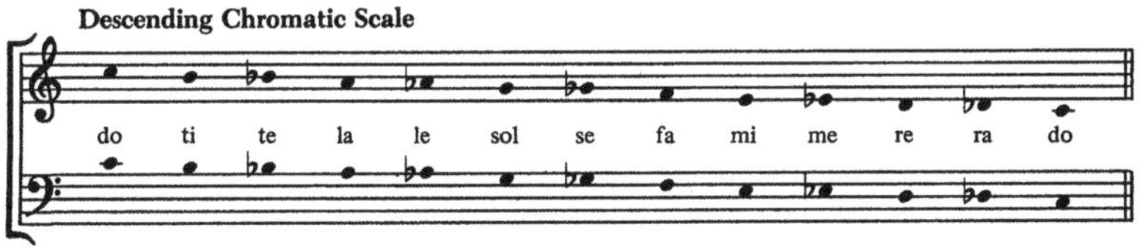

Accidentals

Teaching Suggestions:

Concepts:

- A sharp (♯♩) raises a pitch by a half step.
- A flat (♭♩) lowers a pitch by a half step.
- A natural (♮♩) cancels a previous sharp or flat.
- Introduce solfege syllables for ascending and descending half steps.
- Ascending and descending chromatic scale.

Directions:

- Discuss sharps, flats, naturals, and their functions.
- Carefully study the pitch syllables for altered notes and practice saying them with the correct pronunciation.
- Sing the ascending and descending chromatic scales, concentrating on *good pitch* as well as correct solfege syllables for the altered notes.
- Repeat often, so that recognizing the syllables becomes habit.
- Enharmonic notes are discussed on page 41. You may wish to jump ahead for a brief explanation.
- Maintaining good intonation when singing chromatics is always a challenge. Give the students lots of praise and constant encouragement, and stress alertness at all times.

Practice With Accidentals

Teaching Suggestions:

Concepts:

- Practice with accidentals.
- An accidental covers all notes of the same pitch for an entire measure.
- If an accidental occurs with a note that is tied over a barline, the accidental is not restated for the tied note, but is restated for any following altered notes.
- "Reminder" accidentals.

Directions:

- Review the chromatic scales on p. 39 to become more fluent in the solfege syllables for altered notes.
- Sing examples 1 and 2, and note that they are in different keys (G and C).
- Point out that an accidental applies to all notes of the same pitch for the entire measure, even though the accidental appears only once.
- Point out that a natural is used to cancel a previous sharp or flat.
- Point out the instructions concerning ties over a barline, then sing Example 3. Repeat.

The Accidental Singer

- Study the exercise silently to identify potential trouble spots.
- Point out the "reminder" accidental. Say the pitches in rhythm before singing. Repeat as needed.
- Sing the exercises on solfege syllables. Sing again on a neutral syllable.

40

Practice With Accidentals

If an accidental appears, it affects all following notes of the same pitch in the same measure, even though the accidental is stated only once.

①

②

If an accidental occurs in a tie over a barline, the accidental is not re-stated for the tied note, but should be re-stated for any following altered notes.

③
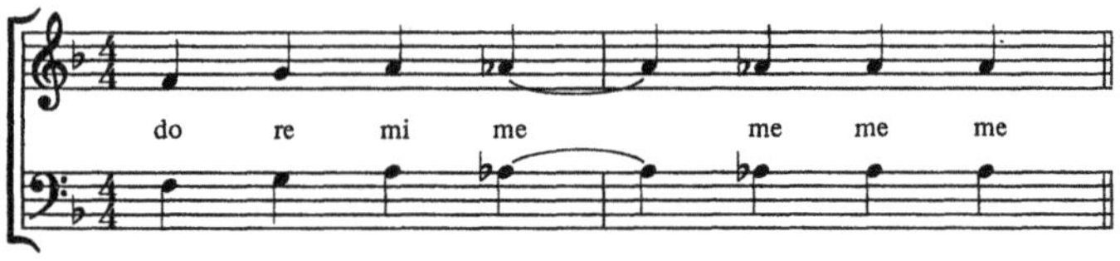

The Accidental Singer

* Many times you will see "reminder" accidentals, although they are not technically necessary.

THE CHORAL APPROACH TO SIGHT-SINGING, VOL. II – Singer's Edition

41

Fun With Accidentals

Notes that look different, but sound the same are called enharmonic notes.

Find some enharmonic notes in the next song.

Accidentals "Ain't" Easy

Chromatic Static!

* For fun, sing with heavy vibrato!

THE CHORAL APPROACH TO SIGHT-SINGING, VOL. II – Singer's Edition

Fun With Accidentals

Teaching Suggestions:

Concepts:

- Enharmonic Notes — Notes that sound the same but are "spelled" differently.
- More practice with accidentals.
- Maintaining good intonation while singing chromatics.
- 6/8 practice

Directions:

Accidentals "Ain't" Easy

- Discuss enharmonic notes, study the examples, and locate examples in the song.
- Say the solfege syllables in rhythm. Repeat. (Boys should use the lower notes in m. 3-4 if possible.)
- Sing the song in solfege. Repeat.
- Add the lyrics. Stress the importance of good intonation. Concentrate!

Chromatic Static

- Count the rhythm, noticing the pick-up note.
- Say the solfege of each line in rhythm.
- Sing each exercise in solfege, parts separately.
- Sing each exercise in solfege, parts together.
- Add the lyrics. Repeat.
- As always, maintaining good intonation will be a challenge. Encourage the singers to always be alert, to concentrate, and give extra attention to avoid flatting.
- Have fun with the special effects!

Songs With Accidentals

Teaching Suggestions:

Concepts:

- Practice with accidentals in a 3-Part song.
- Practice with syncopation.
- Practice with tied rhythms.
- Practice with dotted rhythms.

Directions:

Scott Joplin Sings:

- Point out the tied rhythms and then count aloud. Keep a steady beat and don't rush. Repeat as needed.
- Say the Part I rhythm in solfege, then Part III, then Part II.
- Sing the lines in solfege or on a neutral syllable, individually if necessary, then all together. Repeat as needed.
- The singers will recognize this familiar tune, and knowing it will serve as a self-check for rhythm and pitch. Otherwise, this exercise would be too difficult at this point.

From "The Star Spangled Banner"

- Point out the dotted rhythms in advance and locate the altered notes.
- Establish <u>do</u> and sing all three parts in solfege. If possible, the boys should sing the divisi in the last measure. Repeat as needed.
- Add the lyrics.

NOTE: Check old music textbooks for a complete arrangement, and try to sight-read the whole piece.

42

Songs With Accidentals

Scott Joplin Sings!
(From "The Entertainer")

Sing in solfege.

From "The Star Spangled Banner"

THE CHORAL APPROACH TO SIGHT-SINGING, VOL.II – Singer's Edition

Two Songs

Teaching Suggestions:

Concepts:

- More practice with accidentals, especially the natural sign.
- More practice with sixteenth note patterns, especially:

- Syncopated patterns:

- Form — Sections that are alike or very similar.

Directions:

Hot! (A Hot Time In The Old Town Tonight)

- Locate the difficult rhythms and review how to count them.
- Count the rhythm.
- Look at the pitches and find the place where it goes into harmony.
- Ask how many different altered syllables are there? (Two) Ask if the natural raises or lowers the pitch in this case. (Raises)

Sleep (All Through The Night)

- Ask how many different altered syllables are in this song. (One) Why not two? (The second one is only a reminder accidental and does not alter the pitch.)
- Establish <u>do</u> and sing the song in three parts. Repeat.

Major And Minor

Teaching Suggestions:

Concepts:

- Introduce minor as a la-centered key as compared to major as a do-centered key.
- Introduction to three forms of the minor scale. Songs in minor will be based on one of these three forms of the minor scale.

Directions:

- Read and discuss the explanation of major and minor given in the singer's edition.
- Sing Examples 1 and 2 to compare the sound of major to that of minor.
- Sing the three forms of the minor scale, noting the altered scale tones in Examples 4 and 5.
- Sing the minor scale and chord in different keys. Write examples on the board.
- Practice singing the minor chord and scale before sight-reading or rehearsing a song in minor.

Major And Minor

So far, all the songs and exercises in this book have been written in major keys in which the tonic chord is based on do. There are many songs, however, which are based on "la" and are described as being in a minor key. Sing both examples and hear the differences between the two chords. In order to determine whether a song is in major or minor, look at the last note of the song. If the song ends with do, mi, and sol as the final chord, it is probably major; if it ends with la, do, mi as the final chord, then it probably is minor.

Major Chord

①

Minor Chord

②

Songs in minor often have accidentals, usually either the 6th or 7th notes of the scale. Try these three forms of the minor scale:

Natural Minor

③

Melodic Minor

④

Harmonic Minor

⑤

Major Keys And Their Relative Minor Keys

Major songs take their key name from "do." Since many songs are in a major key, you can usually check the location of "do" and know the name of the key. If the song title says "Sonata in F" they will mean F major, unless otherwise specified.

Minor songs take their key name from "la." As previously stated, they usually end on "la" and usually have several accidentals (especially on the 6th and 7th scale steps, making them "fi" and "si.")

Keys that share the same key signature (same amount of sharps or flats, etc.) are said to be "related." Therefore each major key has a "relative minor key," and each minor key has a "relative major key." To find the name of the relative minor key, look for the letter name of "la." To find the name of the relative major key, look for the letter name of "do." Here are some examples of major keys and their relative minor keys, with a tonic chord (pitch ladder) for each key.

Major Keys And Their Relative Minor Keys

Teaching Suggestions:

Concepts:

- Major keys and their relative minor keys.
- Major keys take their key name from do.
- Minor keys take their key name from la.

Directions:

- Read and discuss the explanation in the singer's edition.
- Sing each major chord, sing down the scale to la, then sing the corresponding relative minor chord. Compare the two chords for their similarities and differences.
- Repeat this process for all the major keys and their relative minors.
- Use the cue-sized notes if possible and/or necessary.

Chord Drills

Teaching Suggestions:

Concepts:

- Chord drills in D minor, G minor, C minor, and F minor.
- Optional 4th part (bass) for changed voices.
- Minor key pitch ladder:

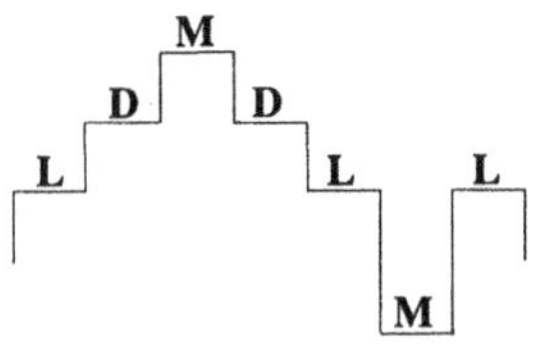

Directions:

- On each exercise, establish do, sing the scale down to la, and sing a minor key tonic chord. This will give structure to the key feeling and help the singers to find their starting pitches.
- Sing each exercise several times in solfege.
- If possible, add the lower 4th (bass) part.
- Refer to this page and the next often for warm-up and tune-up drills, or to help establish a key feeling before sight-reading or rehearsing a song.

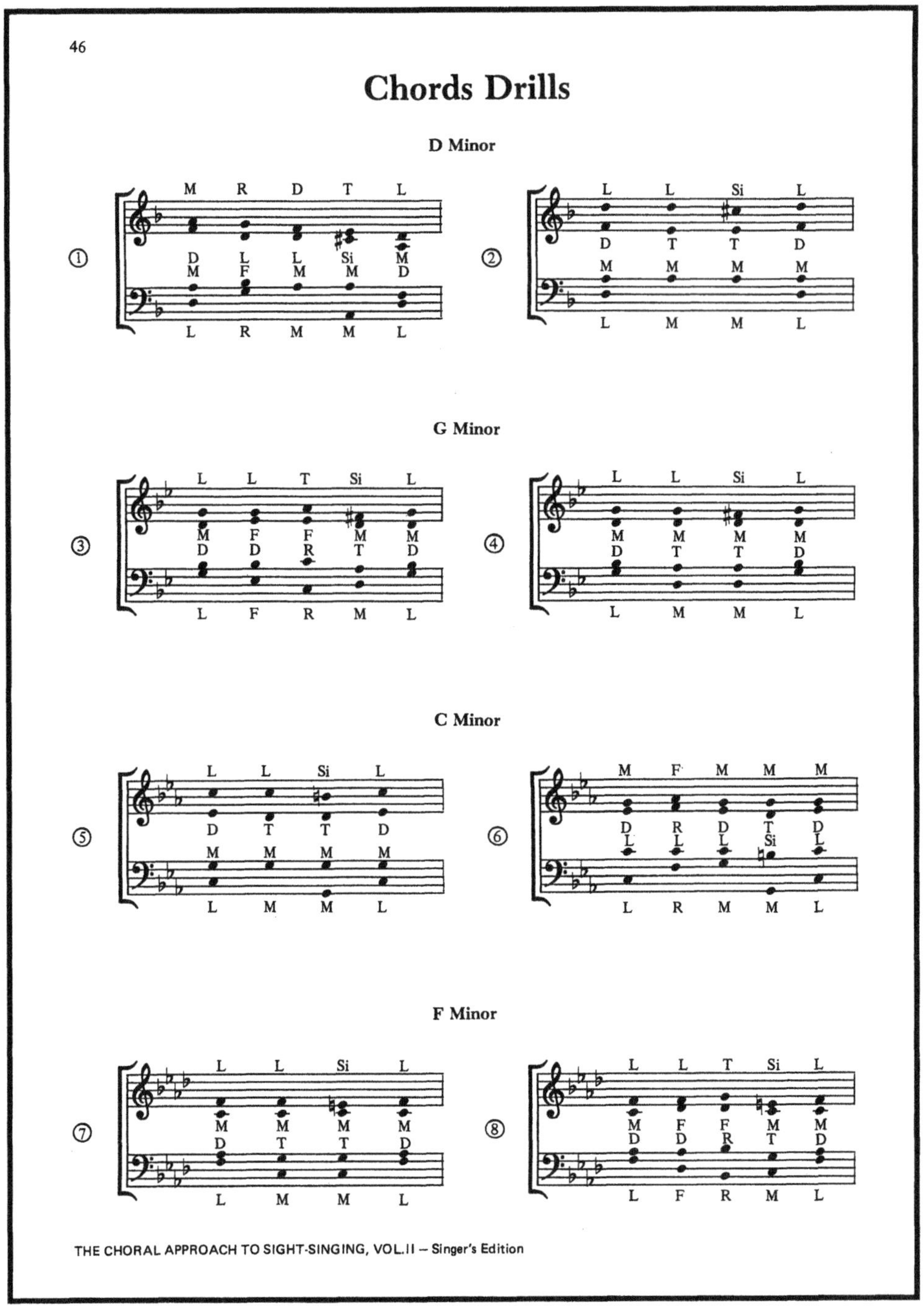

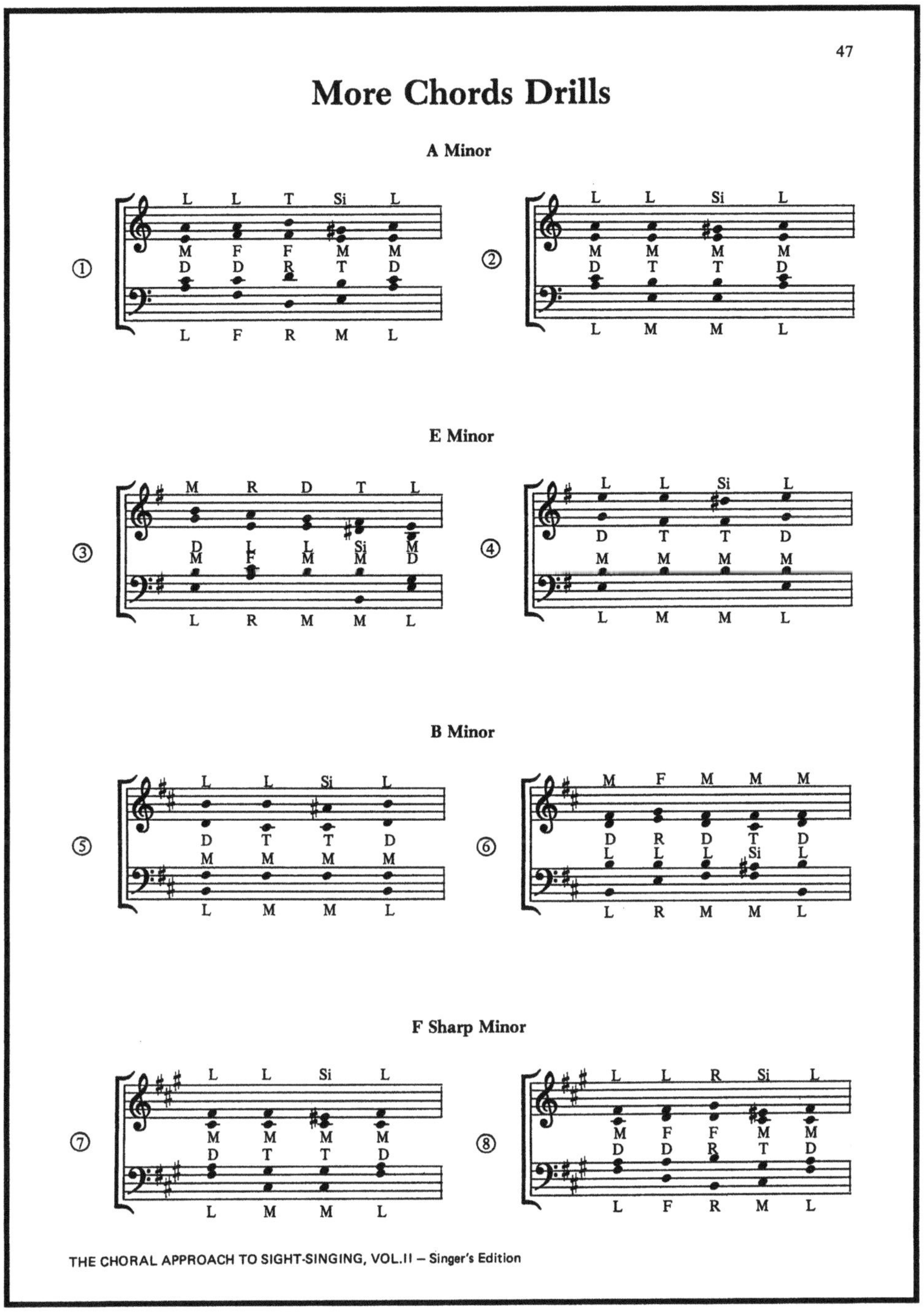

More Chord Drills

Teaching Suggestions:

Concepts:

- Chord drills in A minor, E minor, B minor, and F sharp minor.
- Rapid mental adjustment to key changes and locating do.
- Increased familiarity with minor keys — going past understanding to habit.

Directions:

- Refer to page 48.

Zum Gali Gali

Teaching Suggestions:

Concepts:

- 3-Part a cappella song in a minor key.
- Repeat sign.
- Increased use of dynamics (refer to p. 26).
- Special effects: accent, foot stamp.
- Non-English lyrics. (It is an Israeli work song, and the Hebrew words create a percussive effect that adds to the over-all dynamic quality.

Directions:

- Review the function of the repeat sign. In this song, the repeat sign is used in two different ways. (When you come to a repeat sign, repeat back to the sign facing the opposite direction. If there is none, repeat to the beginning.) Unless otherwise stated, repeat only once.
- Find do, sing the scale down to la, and sing a tonic chord to establish the pitch.
- Sing the song in solfege or a neutral syllable. Observe the dynamics and special effects.
- Add the lyrics.

Pronunciation:

Zum gali
ZOOM GAH-LEE

Hekahlutz le maan
HEH-KAH-LOOTS LEH MAHN

Avodah
AH-VOH-DAH

Songs Without Words

Teaching Suggestions:

Concepts:

- Practice in minor keys.
- 3-Part a cappella songs with an optional 4th part in many places.
- Review accidentals, 3/4 meter, and other musical elements.
- Key relationships

Directions:

- Note the added 4th part option. You may wish to isolate the lower part first, before adding the other parts.
- Look over each song to locate possible difficult spots in advance—accidentals, rhythms in each part not the same, unusual intervals etc.
- Establish <u>do</u>, sing down the scale to <u>la</u>, sing the minor key tonic chord to locate the starting pitches and sing in solfege.
- Repeat as needed, allowing the singers to correct their own mistakes wherever possible.
- Ask the singers to determine the relative major keys of these exercises.

OPTIONAL: Write lyrics to fit the music.

Poor Wayfarin' Stranger

Teaching Suggestions:

Concepts:

- 3-Part a cappella minor song.
- Accidentals, especially the natural sign. In this song, sometimes it raises the pitch and sometimes it lowers the pitch.
- Practice ties, slurs, and dynamics.

Directions:

- Study the song silently and locate the ties and slurs. Review the difference. Notice the places where the parts have different rhythms.
- Identify the key and review the solfege pitches, especially for the altered notes.
- Sing a minor tonic chord and locate the starting pitches.
- If possible, sing the song with the text the first time.
- Allow the singers to silently review their own errors and then repeat.
- Point out the various musical elements (ties, slurs, dynamics) and repeat the song as musically as possible.

We Three Kings

Teaching Suggestions:

Concepts:

- Song in minor that changes to the relative major.
- Practice with accidentals.
- Review of various musical elements: crescendo, decrescendo, dynamic markings, slurs, fermata.

Directions:

- Name the minor key and its relative minor key.
- Sing the minor tonic chord and locate the starting pitches.
- Sing the song in solfege or a neutral syllable, or attempt it complete with lyrics and dynamics.
- Ask the singers to locate where the song changes from minor to major (m. 52).
- Note the fermata and review its function.

NOTES:

52
17
mf
Star of won - der, star of night,
star with roy - al beau - ty bright.
25
cresc.
West - ward lead - ing, still pro - ceed - ing,
decresc.
guide us to thy per - fect light.
THE CHORAL APPROACH TO SIGHT-SINGING, VOL.II – Singer's Edition

Pat-A-Pan

Teaching Suggestions:

Concepts:

- 4-Part a cappella minor song.
- Keeping a steady tempo with repeated rhythm patterns.
- Review musical elements: dynamics, rests.

Directions:

- In the boys' part, notice the repetition — almost an <u>ostinato</u>. Note the places where the lower part changes pitch.
- Sing the song in solfege or on a neutral syllable, or attempt to sight-read it with words and dynamics.
- Correct the errors and repeat as needed.

NOTE: The tendency will be to rush the repeated notes. Concentrate on keeping a good steady tempo.

To improve the diction in the lower part, tell the singers to keep their jaws still and just move their lips.

Russian Rhapsody

Teaching Suggestions:

Concepts:

- 4-Part accompanied minor song.
- Practice with accidentals.
- Song with a tempo change within it.
- Opportunities for contrasts in style and dynamics.

Directions:

- Study the song silently, determining key and meter. Notice the places where the parts do not have the same rhythm and other potential trouble spots.
- Find the spot where the meter changes.
- Practice the rhythm of m. 11-12 so the tempo change does not present a problem.
- Sing a minor tonic chord to establish the key and then sing the starting pitches.
- Sing through slowly in solfege. Repeat, increasing the tempo at m. 12.
- Add the words and dynamics and sing again.
- Finally add the accompaniment and try the alternate suggestion for m. 12—start slowly and do a gradual accellerando to the end.

55
See the leaves a - danc-ing when the wind blows. Loo - lee loo, love-ly
See the leaves a - danc-ing when the wind blows. Loo - lee loo, love-ly
See the leaves a - danc-ing when the wind blows. Loo-lee loo, love-ly
birch tree. Loo - lee loo, love - ly birch tree. Ka -
birch tree. Loo - lee loo, love - ly birch tree. Ka -
birch tree. Loo-lee loo, love - ly birch tree. Ka -
THE CHORAL APPROACH TO SIGHT-SINGING, VOL.II – Singer's Edition

NOTES:

NOTES:

56
12
Faster (♩ = 108) *
lin - ka, ka - lin - ka, ka - lin - ka of mine. In the
lin - ka, ka - lin - ka, ka - lin - ka of mine. In the
lin - ka, ka - lin - ka, ka - lin - ka of mine. In the
12
Faster (♩ = 108) *
gar - den grows a ber - ry, so sweet on the vine. Ka -
gar - den grows a ber - ry, so sweet on the vine. Ka -
gar - den grows a ber - ry, so sweet on the vine. Ka -
* Alternate: Slow with a gradual accellerando to the end.
THE CHORAL APPROACH TO SIGHT-SINGING, VOL.II – Singer's Edition

57
lin - ka, ka - lin - ka, ka - lin - ka of mine. In the gar - den grows a ber - ry, so
lin - ka, ka - lin - ka, ka - lin - ka of mine. In the gar - den grows a ber - ry, so
lin - ka, ka - lin - ka, ka - lin - ka of mine. In the gar - den grows a ber - ry, so
sweet on the vine. Ka - lin - ka, ka - lin - ka, ka - lin - ka of mine. Hey!
sweet on the vine. Ka - lin - ka, ka - lin - ka, ka - lin - ka of mine. Hey!
sweet on the vine. Ka - lin - ka, ka - lin - ka, ka - lin - ka of mine. Hey!
THE CHORAL APPROACH TO SIGHT-SINGING, VOL. II – Singer's Edition

NOTES:

Modulation

Teaching Suggestions:

Concepts:

- Introduce the concept of modulation, or changing from one key to another.
- Finding a "pivot" note in the first key from which to move to the second key.

Directions:

- To introduce the concept of key changes, write the following example on the board for the students to sing.

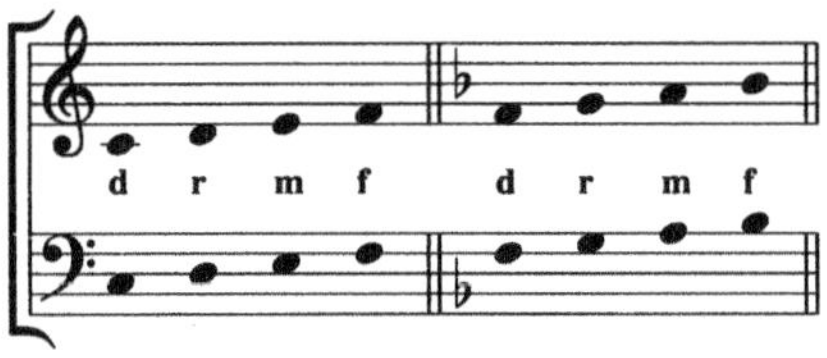

- Try several other examples and let the students suggest notes on which to change keys.
- Read the explanation of modulation in the singer's edition.
- Look at the first example ("When The Saints Go Marching In") and identify the first key and the second key, giving special attention to the pivot note.
- Sing in solfege. Repeat as needed.
- Study the second example ("America The Beautiful"), determine the first key, the second key, and find the pivot note. (Part I pivots on beat 4 of the second measure while Parts II and III pivot on beat 1 of the third measure.
- Sing in solfege. Repeat as needed. Add the words.

Modulation

Sometimes a song changes from one key to another. Usually there will be a new key signature when this happens, but occasionally, the composer will use accidentals. When you are sight-reading in solfege, look ahead for these key changes and decide on a spot to "pivot", or switch into the new key. Look at this fragment of "When The Saints Go Marching In" and notice the pivot note.

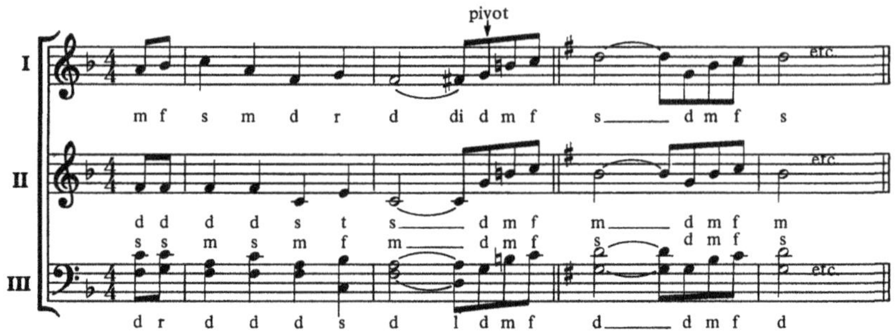

Try another fragment and see if you can determine the first key, the second key and the best spot to pivot.

America The Beautiful

Ev'ry Night

Teaching Suggestions:

Concepts:

- 3-Part a cappella song with a modulation.
- Practice accidentals.
- Practice dynamics, ties, slurs, and sixteenth notes.
- Good opportunity for developing expressive singing.

Directions:

- Read the rhythm of Part I, then Parts II and III. Read the rhythm of all three parts together.
- Study the song silently and locate the possible difficulties. Locate the key change — old key, new key, and determine the best place to pivot. (Part I should pivot in the pick-up to m. 9 and Parts II and III should pivot on beat 1 of m. 9.)
- Read through again in rhythm, this time speaking the solfege syllables.
- Isolate the difficult pitches if necessary (altered notes and movement by chromatics).
- Establish the starting pitches and sing in solfege. Repeat as needed to correct errors.
- Add the words and dynamics and sing as expressively as possible.

Wandering Sharps
What Key Are We In?

Teaching Suggestions:

Concepts:

- Practice with accidentals and key changes.

Directions:

Wandering Sharps

- This short example changes keys three times. Pivot on beat 1 of the measure of the key change.
- Notice how the chord before the key change leads into the new key.
- Sing in solfege. Repeat as needed. Concentrate on good intonation.

What Key Are We In?

- While the key center of this example might be ambiguous, sing the entire example in solfege for the key of B flat.
- There are some challenging intervals in this example, but they provide good ear-training practice.
- Sing through in solfege. Repeat as needed.

Keep On Traveling

Teaching Suggestions:

Concepts:

- 4-Part accompanied song with a modulation.
- Review syncopation and eighth-note pick-ups.
- Repeat sign, 1st and 2nd endings.

Directions:

- Study the rhythm silently and then count aloud, keeping a steady beat and concentrating on precision. Isolate the syncopated patterns, if necessary.
- Look over the key structure and find the modulation. What is the first key, the second key and where is the best place to pivot? (Pick-ups to m. 12)
- Read through the rhythm in solfege. Repeat as needed.
- Establish the starting pitches and sing in solfege. Repeat as needed to correct errors.
- Add the words and sing again.
- Add the accompaniment and try to increase the tempo. Repeat with all the dynamics.

Congratulate the students heartily on their accomplishments as they have finished the book and encourage them to "keep on traveling" down the road to musical literacy, as well!!!

NOTES:

62
Keep on trav - el - ing that heav'n - ly road.
Join the right - eous in that heav'n - ly band.
Keep on trav - el - ing that heav'n - ly road.
Join the right - eous in that heav'n - ly band.
Keep on trav - el - ing that heav'n - ly road.
Join the right - eous in that heav'n - ly band.
Keep on trav - el - ing that heav'n - ly road,
Join the right-eous in that heav'n - ly band,
sing - ing "Glo - ry, hal - le -
Keep on trav - el - ing that heav'n - ly road,
Join the right-eous in that heav'n - ly band,
sing - ing "Glo - ry, hal - le -
Keep on trav - el - ing that heav'n - ly road,
Join the right-eous in that heav'n - ly band,
sing - ing "Glo - ry, hal - le -
THE CHORAL APPROACH TO SIGHT-SINGING, VOL.II – Singer's Edition

63
1.
2.
12
lu!" 2. We're gon-na lu!" We're gon-na shout for glo-ry in that
joy - ous morn. Shout for glo-ry in that joy - ous morn.
THE CHORAL APPROACH TO SIGHT-SINGING, VOL. II – Singer's Edition

NOTES:

NOTES:

64
Shout for glo - ry in that joy - ous morn, sing - ing "Glo - ry
Shout for glo - ry in that joy - ous morn, sing -ing "Glo - ry
Shout for glo - ry in that joy - ous morn, sing-ing "Glo - ry
opt. div.
hal - le - lu."
opt. div.
hal - le - lu."
hal - le - lu."
THE CHORAL APPROACH TO SIGHT-SINGING, VOL.II – Singer's Edition

TERMS AND SYMBOLS

I. DYNAMICS (loudness and softness)

pp - (pianissimo) (pee-ah-NEE-see-moh) - very soft
p - (piano) (pee-AH-noh) - soft
mp - (mezzo piano) (MEH-tsoh) - medium soft
mf - (mezzo forte) - medium loud
f - (forte) (FOR-teh) - loud
ff - (fortissimo) (for-TEE-see-moh) - very loud

crescendo (*cresc.* <) (kreh-SHEN-doh) - gradually louder

decrescendo (*decresc.* >) (deh-kreh-SHEN-doh) - gradually softer

diminuendo (*dim.*) (dih-min-new-EN-doh) - gradually softer

accent (>) - stress the note by singing it louder.

II. TEMPO (TEM-poh) - the speed of the beat

accellerando (*accel.*) (ah-chel-leh-RAHN-doh) - gradually faster

rallentando (*rall.*) (rahl-en-TAHN-doh) - gradually slower

ritardando (*rit.* or *ritard.*) (ree-tahr-DAHN-doh) - gradually slower

fermata 𝄐 (fur-MAH-tah) - hold the note for longer than its value; the length is left up to the interpretation of the director.

metronome marking (♩= 100) - a marking which appears over the first staff of music which indicates the kind of note which will get the beat, and the number of beats per minute as measured by a metronome.

rubato (roo-BAH-toh) - the tempo is free; left up to the interpretation of the director

style word - a marking which appears over the first staff of music, which indicates either the tempo or the way (style) the music is to be sung.

Largo (LAHR-goh) - very slow
Adagio (ah-DAH-jee-oh) - slow
Andante (ahn-DAHN-teh) - medium
Moderato (mah-deh-RAH-toh) - medium
Allegro (ah-LEH-groh) -fast
Vivace (vee-VA-cheh) - very fast
Presto (PREH-stoh) - very fast

A Tempo (ah TEM-poh) - return to the original tempo (speed)

III. OTHER TERMS AND SYMBOLS

coda (KOH-dah) - ending

Da capo (D. C.) (dah KAH-poh) - repeat from the beginning

D.C. al fine (ahl-FEE-neh) - repeat from the beginning to "fine" (end)

Dal Segno (D.S.) (dahl SAYN-yoh) - go back to the sign 𝄋 and repeat

D.S. al fine (ahl FEE-neh) - repeat from the sign 𝄋 to "fine" (end)

divisi (*div.*) (dee-VEE-see) - divide, the part divides

legato (leh-GAH-toh) - smoothly connected, may be connected by a slur

molto (MOHL-toh) - much, very (molto rit.)

poco (POH-koh) - little (poco cresc.)

repeat - 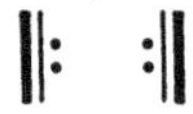 repeat the section. If the first repeat sign is omitted, go back to the beginning

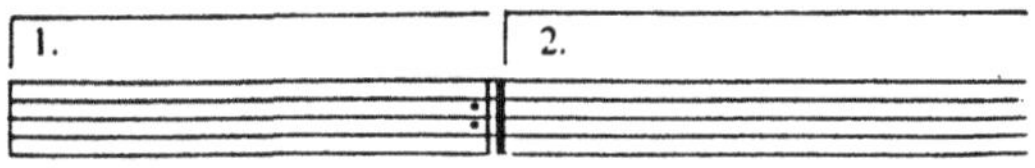

First and Second Endings: At the end of the first ending (bracket 1), repeat, but skip the first ending and go to the second ending (bracket 2).

sempre (SEHM-preh) - always and the next time through ex; sempre forte = always loud.

simile (SIM-eh-leh) - continue in the same way

staccato (♩) (stah-KAH-toh) - short, separated notes

’ - take a breath

n.b. (no breath) and ⌒ (dotted slur) - Do not breathe here

IV. PITCH

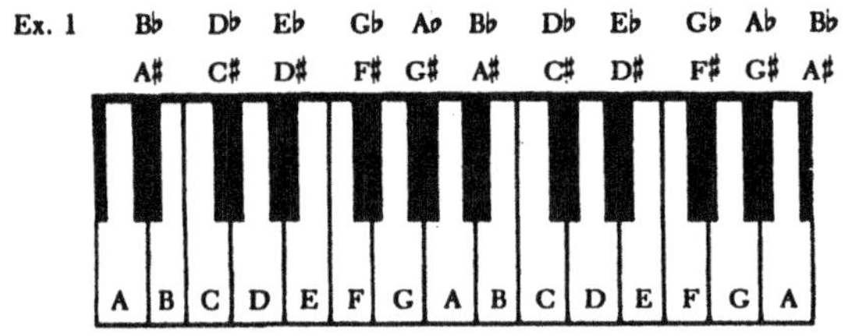

V. SYLLABLES

MOVABLE DO

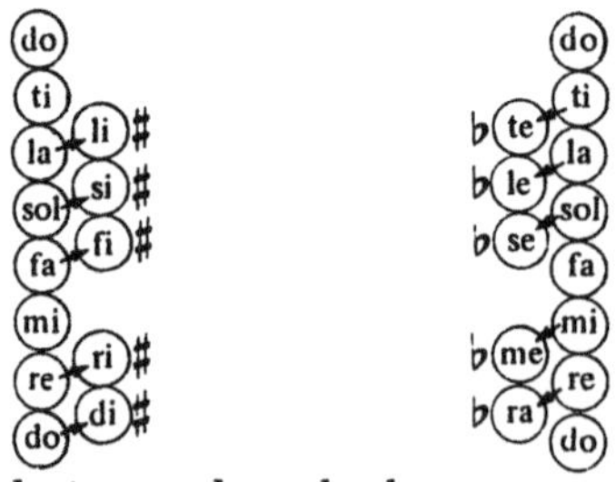

In movable do, do is designated as the home tone (or tonic) in every key.

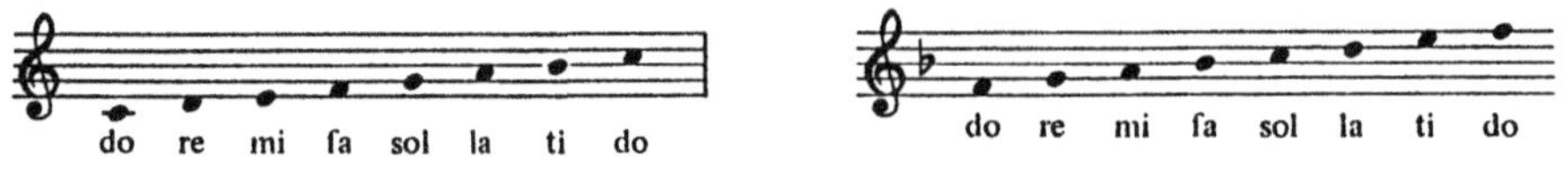

PATTERNS OF SOUND has been written using movable do.

FIXED DO

In fixed do, C is always do, no matter what the key.

Ex. 1

do di re ri mi fa fi sol si la li ti do

Ex. 2

do ti te la le sol se fa mi me re ra do

In fixed do, keys other than C retain their fixed location, and use the altered pitch syllables.

fa sol la (te) do re mi fa

sol la ti do re mi (fi) sol

NUMBERS

Numbers can be used instead of the syllables in movable do.

do	=	8
ti	=	7
la	=	6
sol	=	5
fa	=	4
mi	=	3
re	=	2
do	=	1

VI. **RHYTHM** - the organization of non-pitched sounds in time

♩ (ta) - quarter note	𝄽 - quarter rest
𝅗𝅥 (ta-a) - half note	𝄼 - half rest
𝅗𝅥. (ta-a-a) - dotted half note	𝄼. - dotted half rest
𝅝 (ta-a-a-a) - whole note	𝄻 - whole rest (may also refer to an empty measure)
♫ ti ti (or ♪ ♪ ti ti) - eighth notes	𝄾 - eighth rest
𝅘𝅥𝅯𝅘𝅥𝅯𝅘𝅥𝅯𝅘𝅥𝅯 ti ki ti ki (or 𝅘𝅥𝅯 𝅘𝅥𝅯 𝅘𝅥𝅯 𝅘𝅥𝅯 ti ki ti ki) - sixteenth notes	𝄿 - sixteenth rest

Dots - a dot lengthens a note by half its value

VII. **METER** - Meter refers to the grouping of beats.

A meter signature or time signature indicates the grouping with two numbers:

4/4 3/4 2/4 6/8

The top number indicates the number of beats per measure and the bottom number indicates the kind of note getting the beat.

GLOSSARY

Absolute Pitch - The letter names of the notes (see PITCH, p. 68).

A Cappella - (ah-kah-PEH-lah) Singing without instrumental accompaniment.

Accent - Stress of emphasize a note by singing it louder.

Accidentals - Symbols that move the pitch up or down a half step.

♯ - sharp - raises the pitch one half step

♭ - flat - lowers the pitch one half step

♮ - natural - cancels a previous sharp or flat. (When it cancels a flat, the pitch is raised one half step; when it cancels a sharp, the pitch is lowered one half step).

Accidentals affect all notes of the same pitch that follow the accidental within the same measure, or if an altered note is tied over a barline.

Bar - See measure.

Barline - A vertical line to separate measures. A double bar indicates the end of a song.

Barline **Double Bar**

Beat - The unit of pulse in music.

Chord - Three or more pitches sounding at the same time or in a pitch ladder (broken chord). Common chords used at this level include:

Numerous other examples are built on other scale steps, or involve accidentals, and will become more common as you gain sight-reading competency.

Chromatic - Moving up or down by half steps (See PITCH, p. 68).

Clef - The symbol at the beginning of the staff.

TREBLE CLEF
Used for higher voices and instruments, and the piano right hand. The curve is wrapped around the G, so it is also called the G clef.

BASS CLEF
Used for lower voices and instruments and the piano left hand. The two dots are on either side of F, so it is often referred to as the F clef.

Coda - See OTHER TERMS AND SYMBOLS, p. 67

Common Time - 4/4 meter indicated in the time signature with the symbol "C".

Cut Time - Technically it is 2/2 time, but it is really 4/4 time where the half note gets the beat. It is marked with the symbol ₵ (common time cut in half).

Da Capo - See OTHER TERMS AND SYMBOLS, p. 67

Dal Segno - See OTHER TERMS AND SYMBOLS, p. 67

Diatonic - Step by step movement within a regular scale (any key).

Divisi - *(div.)* Divide, the part divides.

Downbeat - The (accented) first beat of the measure.

Enharmonic - Notes with more than one name. For instance, F♯ and G♭ are the same note, they are "enharmonic" with each other. Di and ra are enharmonic, etc.

Fermata - See TEMPO, p.

Fine - See OTHER TERMS AND SYMBOLS, p.

Flat - ♭ See ACCIDENTALS. Flat also refers to faulty intonation, when the notes are sung or played slightly under the correct pitch.

G Clef - 𝄞 See CLEF, p.70

Half Step - The interval between notes of a chromatic scale. (do - di, re - ri, etc. and F - F♯, A♭ - G, etc.)

Harmony - Two or more musical tones sounding at the same time.

Interval - The distance between two pitches.

Intonation - Accuracy of pitch.

Key - The organization of tonality around a single pitch (key-note). Scales have relationships between scale steps that remain constant even when the key-note moves. In solfege, the key-note is do in major and la in minor (see KEY-NOTE AND KEY SIGNATURE).

Key-Note - The pitch which is the tonal center of a key. The first tone (degree) of a scale. It is also called the "tonic." A key is named after the key-note; for example in the key of A♭, A♭ is the key-note. (See KEY AND KEY SIGNATURE).

Key Signature - The group of sharps or flats at the beginning of a staff which combine to indicate the locations of the key-note. If there are no sharps or flats, the key is automatically C major or A minor, and do is located:

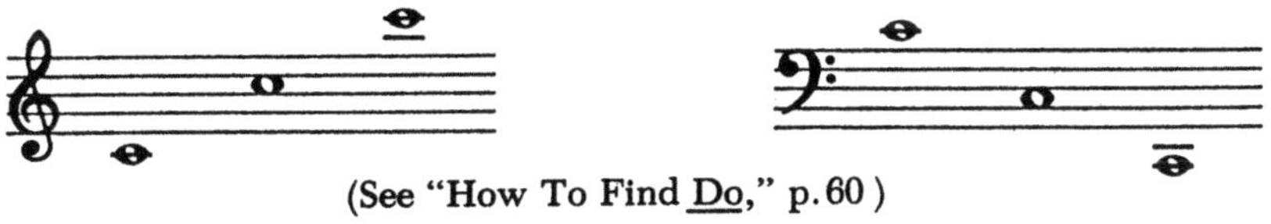

(See "How To Find Do," p.60)

Legato - See OTHER TERMS AND SYMBOLS, p. 68

Ledger Lines - The short lines used to extend the lines and spaces of the staff. (Sometimes spelled "leger" lines)

Major Key/Scale/Mode - A tonality in which the key-note is do and the half and whole step pattern of the scale is:

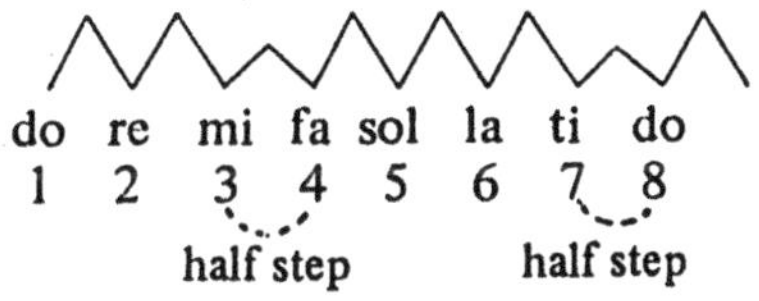

Measure - A group of beats divided by barlines. Measures are sometimes called bars. The first beat of each measure is accented.

Melody - A succession of musical tones; also the predominant line in a song.

Meter - The grouping of beats. (See METER, p.69)

Meter Signature - See METER, p. 69)

Middle C - The C which is located closest to the middle of the piano keyboard. Middle C can be written in either treble or bass clef.

These two notes are enharmonic (same note) (see enharmonic)

Minor Key/Mode/Scale - A tonality in which the key-note is la, and the half/whole step pattern of the scale is:

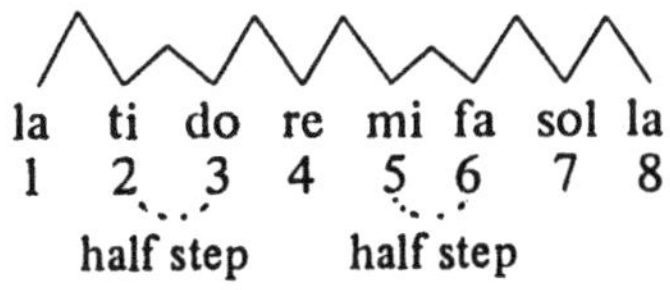

Accidentals are frequently used in a minor key, most often after fi and si.

Modulation - Changing keys in the middle of a song. Adjust to the key signature, the key-note, and proceed.

Natural - See ACCIDENTALS, p. 70)

Notation - All written notes and symbols which are used to represent music.

Octave - The interval between two notes of the same name:

Pick-Up - An incomplete measure at the beginning of a song, usually one or two notes. The last measure should be correspondingly shorter.

Pitch - The highness or lowness of musical sounds.

Pitch Ladder - See TONIC CHORD, p. 72

Relative Major/Minor - Major and minor tonalities which share the same key signature.

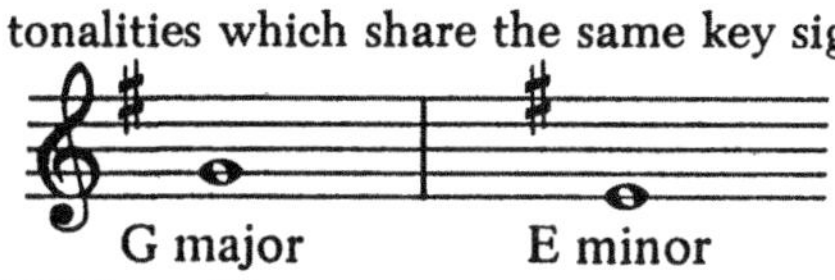

Repeat - See OTHER TERMS AND SYMBOLS, p. 68

Rhythm - The organization of non-pitched sounds in time. (To avoid confusion, beat is "the steady pulse in music," while rhythm is "the way the words go.")

Scale - An arrangement of successive pitches in a set order or pattern to indicate tonality.

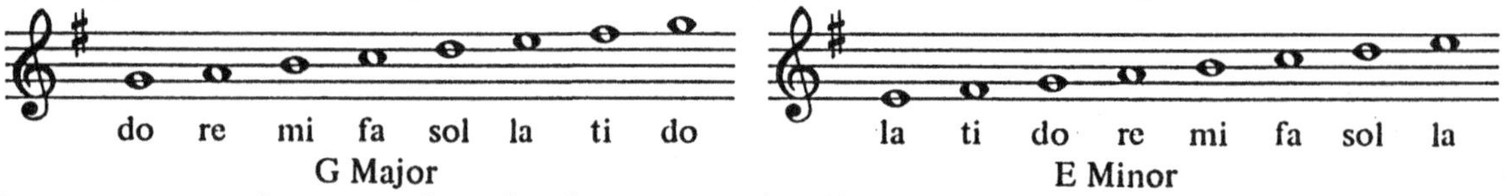

Score - The arrangement of a group of vocal and instrumental staffs which all sound at the same time.

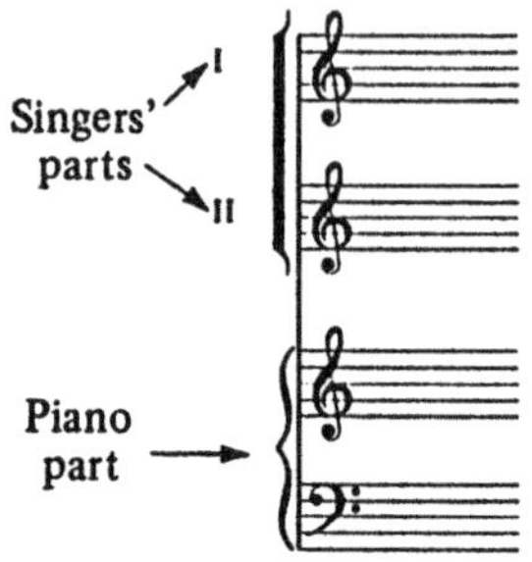

Sequence - The successive repetition of a short melodic idea at different pitch levels.

Sharp - ♯ See ACCIDENTALS; also, faulty intonation in which the note is sung slightly above the correct pitch.

Skip - The melodic movement of one note to another in intervals larger than a step.

Slur - See p. 42

Solfege (sohl-FEZH) or solfeggio (sohl-FEJ-ee-oh) - The study of sight-singing using pitch syllables (do re mi, etc.)

Staccato - See OTHER TERMS AND SYMBOLS, p. 68

Staff - The five horizontal parallel lines on which notes are placed to show pitch.

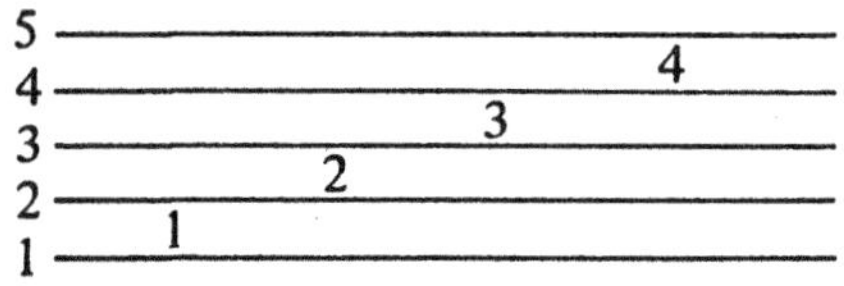

The lines and spaces are numbered from the bottom up.

Step - Melodic movement from one note to the next higher or lower scale degree.

Syllables - Names given to pitch units or rhythm units to aid in sight-reading.

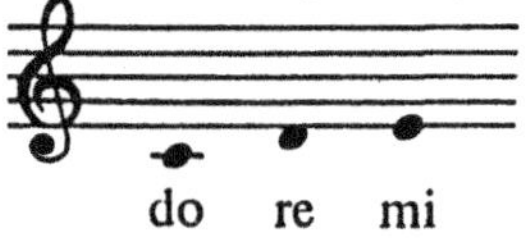

Syncopation - The use of accents in irregular places to create rhythmic interest. This is briefly discussed on p. . Other examples include:

Tempo - See TEMPO, p.

Tie - See p. 40

Time Signature - See METER, p. 69

Tonality - The organization of pitches in a song in which a certain pitch (tone) is designated as the "key-note" or the note which is the tonal center of a key.

Tone - A musical sound of definite pitch and quality.

Tonic - The key-note of a key or scale.

Tonic Chord - The name given to the chord built on the key-note of the scale (pitch ladder).

Transpose - To re-write or perform a song in a key other than the original.

Treble Clef - 𝄞 See CLEF, p. 70

Triad - See CHORD, p. 70

Triplet - Three notes of the same value which are equal in duration to two notes of the same value.

Unison - All parts singing the same notes at the same time, (or singing in octaves).

Whole Step - Two half steps.